HUGH MACLENNAN

STUDIES IN CANADIAN LITERATURE

General Editors: Hugo McPherson, Gary Geddes

HUGH MACLENNAN

George Woodcock

The Copp Clark Publishing Company

The author is editor of the magazine *Canadian Literature,*
and the author of many books; his most recent critical
work is *The Crystal Spirit: a Study of George Orwell.*
He is a fellow of the Royal Society of Canada and won
the Governor General's Award for literature in 1966.

[1639]

Excerpts from the works of Hugh MacLennan are re-
printed through the courtesy of the following:
from *Two Solitudes, The Watch That Ends the Night,
Return of the Sphinx, Thirty and Three,* by permission
of The Macmillan Company of Canada Limited;
from *Scotchman's Return and Other Essays,* by permission of the author, The Macmillan Company of Canada
Limited, and Charles Scribner's Sons, New York;
from *Each Man's Son,* by permission of The Macmillan
Company of Canada Limited and Little, Brown and Co.,
Boston;
from *Barometer Rising,* Copyright 1941, by permission
of Duell, Sloan and Pearce, affiliate of Meredith Press,
and The Canadian Publishers, McClelland and Stewart
Limited, Toronto;
from *Cross Country* and *The Precipice,* by permission of
the author.

CONTENTS

ABBREVIATIONS

BR   *Barometer Rising.* Toronto: McClelland and Stewart, New Canadian Library, undated. (c. 1960.)

CC   *Cross Country.* Toronto: Collins, 1949.

CO   *The Colour of Canada.* Toronto: McClelland and Stewart, 1967.

EM   *Each Man's Son.* Toronto: Macmillan, 1951.

O   *Oxyrhynchus.* Amsterdam: Hackert, 1968.

P   *The Precipice.* Toronto: Collins, 1948.

RS   *Return of the Sphinx.* Toronto: Macmillan, 1967.

SR   *Scotchman's Return and Other Essays.* Toronto: Macmillan, 1960.

TS   *Two Solitudes.* Toronto: Collins, White Circle Pocket Edition, undated. (c. 1950.)

TT   *Thirty and Three.* Toronto: Macmillan, 1954.

WE   *The Watch that Ends the Night.* Toronto: Macmillan, 1959.

7R   *Seven Rivers of Canada.* Toronto: Macmillan, 1961.

I

INTRODUCTION

Hugh MacLennan occupies a position of uneasy eminence in Canadian letters. He is probably the most considerable novelist our country has yet produced, yet this is a statement one can make only to the accompaniment of elaborate qualifications. Other novelists—Mazo de la Roche and Morley Callaghan in particular—have received a louder international acclaim; yet others, like Thomas B. Costain and Ralph Connor, have in their time enjoyed a wider popularity and a greater share of the rewards that go to the habitual best-seller. Moreover, during the past generation a fair company of individual novels have appeared that are aesthetically superior to the best Mac-Lennan has written: Malcolm Lowry's *Under the Volcano*, Sinclair Ross's *As for Me and My House*, Brian Moore's *Lonely Passion of Judith Hearne*, Mordecai Richler's *The Apprenticeship of Duddy Kravitz* and Ethel Wilson's *Equations of Love* come immediately to mind.

Yet because of the nature of the task he has set himself—the fictional delineation of a nation's odyssey—Mac-Lennan assumes a largeness (which is not necessarily the same as a greatness) of a kind rivalled in Canada only by another common man tortured by the immanence of genius, Frederick Philip Grove. It is the same kind of largeness as characterized the great Russian novelists, and if neither MacLennan nor Grove has produced a work to compare even distantly with *War and Peace,* they have both been touched with the sense of space and history, and of man in relation to both, that characterizes Tolstoy. No novel by MacLennan is, at best, more than a flawed masterpiece. Yet so many grand imperfects add up to a body of work which makes most Canadian critics agree, uneasily and often against their wills, that MacLennan is the most significant of our novelists, and that he is so not because of the originality with which he has handled the art of fiction—for in form he is conservative—but rather in the original way he has presented his vision of the Canadian condition to his fellow countrymen and to the world at large.

For MacLennan is unashamedly a didactic writer; he is seeking, like Tolstoy, to teach us social truths through the credible encounters of human beings. And it is this persistent didacticism that I take as the justification for the form I have given to this study. I begin with a cluster of chapters not on MacLennan the novelist, but on his literary *alter ego,* MacLennan the essayist, partly with the intention of giving a needed prominence to an aspect of MacLennan's work insufficiently considered by most critics but even more because of the extent to which a consideration of the essays will illuminate the novels.

MacLennan himself has said some interesting things about the place of his essays in the general pattern of his work. They were almost all written for magazines like *The Montrealer, Saturday Night* and *Maclean's;* they represent MacLennan as the man of letters writing for regular money that would give him the leisure to write novels. But they are much more than mere occasional journalism. In the preface to his first collection of essays,

Cross Country, MacLennan remarks on the functions the essays fulfilled at a time when he was also working continuously on his novels. Given his itch to teach, in print as well as in the classroom, they granted intellectual relief by providing a quicker way to put an urgent argument than a novel would provide; at the same time, they helped MacLennan to work out problems that had to be solved before he could "advance with my principal work, the writing of novels" (*CC,* vii). They also served his mind, stimulated to proliferating thought by the process of creation, in enabling him to develop "all manner of things that fascinate and delight" (*CC,* viii) for which his novels gave neither scope nor room.

The results of these necessities have been three volumes of miscellaneous essays on things profound and trivial (*Cross Country, Thirty and Three* and *Scotchman's Return*) and two volumes (*Seven Rivers of Canada* and *The Colour of Canada*) in which MacLennan describes and evokes his country, historically and through the five senses. The essays stand in their own right as urbane and appealing examples of a literary form little practiced either in this age or in Canada. The best of them are more complete realizations of intent, more flawless examples of literary art than any of MacLennan's novels, which does not mean that they are more important, for the grandeur of effort that gives stature to the best of the novels is never there; they are fine small works and pretend to be no more.

Indeed, even for the reader, their lasting interest, after the first pleasure of reading an excellent piece of prose, is likely to be in the background they provide for the novels. They contain the scattered statements and reminiscences

3

out of which it is possible to frame a good intellectual autobiography of the author as a young and—somewhat less fully—as a middle-aged man. They provide the material on which we can establish MacLennan's philosophy of life and his view of the place within it of the literary art. Finally, the essays introduce us to that historic vision of the Canadian nation at its time of flowering and crisis which preoccupies MacLennan and which, dominating his novels, gives them both their vitality and their flaws.

I shall therefore begin, mainly using information provided by MacLennan in his essays, to trace as much of his life as is meaningful for the better knowledge of his works. I shall next consider the essays as statements on life, on art and on history. Only then, in the larger and later part of the study, shall I proceed to consider MacLennan as novelist. This procedure is justified by the dual aspects of MacLennan's role—as essayist and as novelist—and by the openly didactic nature of his fiction. He sets out frankly to teach, and if we can learn before we begin to study his novels the lessons he is intending to impart, we shall be all the freer to assess his books for the quality of their fictional craft and art as distinct from the appropriateness of the doctrines they are shaped to project.

II

SKETCH FOR A LIFE

Hugh MacLennan has described himself as "three-quarters Scotch, and Highland at that" (*SR*, 1) and an eighth loyalist; the remaining fraction he has not chosen publicly to identify. But it is the Scottish three-quarters that he has always regarded as the most important in determining his nature, in endowing him with Gaelic apprehensions, with a tendency towards foreboding, with a habit of intuitively assessing other people.

He was born in 1907 at Glace Bay in Nova Scotia. His father, a doctor in a Cape Breton coal mining community, spoke in Gaelic as easily as in lilting Highland English. Dr. MacLennan was a third generation Nova Scotian, yet his son remembered him as entirely Scottish in his outlook and in his response to life.

> All the perplexity and doggedness of the race was in him, its loneliness, tenderness and affection, its deceptive vitality, its quick flashes of violence, its dog-whistle sensitivity to sounds to which Anglo-Saxons are stone-deaf, its incapacity to tell its heart to foreigners save in terms foreigners do not comprehend, its resigned indifference to whether they comprehend or not. (*SR*, 1)

MacLennan's grandfather and his grandfather's father had also been born on Cape Breton. His grandfather's grandfather had come from the Highlands in the early years of the nineteenth century, a member of a weak clan with a loud tartan whose war cry was suitably pessimistic, "The Ridge of Tears." The Highland clans had declined because their enemies were stronger, but even more because their organization was primitively tribal and their economy was backward and outdated. Returning belatedly—at the age of 51—to the land of his ancestors and to the place of Kintail from which they came, MacLennan realised their historical predicament from the very shape of the land out of which they had wrung their meagre existence. "Often I have said to myself that my grandfathers three times removed lived in a culture as primitive as Homer's, and last summer in the Highlands I knew that they really had," he wrote in 1959 (SR, 10).

Defeated by the English, dispossessed by their own feudal leaders who chose to become British gentlemen rather than Scottish clan chieftains, the highland crofters and fishermen sailed the Atlantic in the holds of the emigrant ships. By right of endeavour they became the third of those whom we call Canada's founding (as distinct from native) peoples; the French Canadians had settled Lower Canada and the Loyalists set the British imprint on the Maritime Provinces and on Lower Canada, but it was the Highland Scots who were hardy enough to dominate the fur trade on the frontiers beyond civilization, and to lead the great journeys to the Pacific that established a claim over the west by which it was saved to become an eventual part of Canada. "What Scotland lost," remarked MacLennan for whom the role of his people has become an inspiring myth, "Canada was to gain" (7R, 117).

With their hardiness and their Gaelic melancholia, the Highlanders brought with them the harsh Presbyterian faith of John Knox and the Calvinist guilt bred of a conviction that men were born in original sin and only the capricious grace of election could save a few of them. MacLennan's father was deeply marked by the gloom of his inherited religion, and it was "his Calvinist way to permit himself to be comfortable only when things were going badly" (*CC*, 29). He combined this religious sense of the appropriateness of misfortune with a remnant of Gaelic superstition that made him distrust good luck, and his son records that in 1929, when he received the unexpected news that he had been awarded a Rhodes scholarship, his father sent him out—despite the fact that it was Sabbath—to placate the diffused malevolence of the universe by shovelling snow.

Yet, as Calvinist households went, that of the MacLennans was not unrelievedly strict. The novelist remembers in his childhood little of the puritan feeling that pleasure was intrinsically sinful, and he portrays his father as a man with a deep and lyrical passion for learning, an amateur classicist who would read Latin and Greek texts in the original for pleasure and enjoyed exercising his mind on the complexities of philosophy.

If the Highlanders left in Scotland a poverty that verged on famine, in Nova Scotia they found a land almost as harsh and rocky as their own, a land that impressed MacLennan even as a child as manifestly intractable. Of his early years in Glace Bay there is little that he records directly, though memories flashing out of that first childhood helped to create the atmospheric background to his novel of Cape Breton life, *Each Man's Son*.

When he was six his father went away for a year of study; when he was seven the family moved to Halifax; and it was this small town which events in 1914 dragged into the path of history that dominated MacLennan's formative years. He did not leave Halifax or travel far away from it until he was twenty-two.

Not only in his novel, *Barometer Rising*, but also in his essays there are finely evocative passages devoted to the vanished Dickensian city, largely destroyed in the great explosion of 1917, which he first encountered with a shock of admiration when he came there in 1914 with his parents and "stood on a corner watching one of those crazy little street cars bucking along Barrington Street" (*CC*, 96). "Portrait of a City," in *Cross Country*, is an eloquent prose ode to the city of his youth, but there is a more intimate appeal, which skilfully skirts the edge of sentimentality, in the Christmas tale, "An Orange from Portugal."

There were dingy basement kitchens all over the town where rats were caught every day. The streets were full of teamsters, hard-looking men with lean jaws, most of them, and at the entrance to the old North Street Station cab drivers in long coats would mass behind a heavy anchor chain and terrify travellers with bloodcurdling howls as they bid for fares. Whenever there was a south-east wind, harbour bells moaned behind the wall of fog that cut the town off from the rest of the world. Queer faces peered at you suddenly from doorways set flush with the streets. When a regiment held a smoker in the old Masonic Hall you could see a line beginning to form in the

8

early morning, waiting for the big moment at mid-night when the doors would be thrown open to the town and any man could get a free drink who could reach the hogsheads. (CC, 23-24)

It was a town of extraordinary contrasts between the dour puritanism of many of its inhabitants and the sordid Alsatia of the waterside streets; a town where "the pompous importers . . . stalked to church on Sunday mornings, swinging their canes" and oblivious of "the waifs and strays and beachcombers and discharged soldiers and sailors whom the respectable never seemed to notice" but who helped to make up the "deplorable and marvellous" city that stirred the imagination of the boy from Cape Breton and gave him for the first time that sense of the wonder of human existence which helped to shape him into a novelist.

Not only the wonder of human existence, but also the cruelty. For quickly the war cast its shadow over the boy's developing consciousness. On Christmas Eve, 1915, his father went overseas, stepping out from the family house and joining the tail of the marching columns that wound through the town gathering the men like a constantly growing snake. Later he read of the gas attack at Ypres, and "realised for the first time that the outer world could be awful." And, in 1917, while he was still at grammar school, he was witness to the event that haunted his mind until, in his first successful novel, he could at last exorcise it by giving it imaginative form.

One cold, clear December morning, while the boys were playing in the packed ashes about the school, and the first fight of the day was brewing, there was

9

a roar past all hearing, and we saw the windows of the school burst inward and the trees toss, and a teacher stagger out the front door with blood streaming from her face. During the following hours as the sky darkened first with smoke, then with clouds, and finally with the snow of a driving blizzard, we saw the north end of the city in flames and the dead and wounded streaming south on slovens, ash and garbage carts, wagons, cars, baby carriages, trucks, ambulances, in anything that would roll. (CC, 101)

Halifax was half destroyed by the great explosion when the French munition ship *Mont Blanc* took fire in a collision and blew up in the harbour. Yet this experience merely intensified a sense of identity with embattled England and ravaged Europe, an identity increased with every contingent of troops that marched through the streets and every transport that set out in convoy across the Atlantic.

But it was not merely in wartime that Haligonians looked eastward. Their ancestors had accepted Confederation only with reluctance, and the loss of prosperity through the decline of ship-building and of the great Nova Scotian sailing fleet (once the world's fourth largest merchant fleet), coinciding with their first decades as a province of Canada, had given them little enthusiasm for the new Dominion. The union, in fact, was no more than political; emotionally, and even economically, Nova Scotia was still not a part of Canada. "I grew up in invincible ignorance about so many things," MacLennan has remarked (TT, 30), and among those many things was the whole of the Dominion west of Nova Scotia.

Like his fellow Nova Scotians, he looked eastward if he looked anywhere outside his native province, and it was London that seemed the metropolis of his world. Given his upbringing, it was natural that when he had passed through Mr. Strickland's Academy for young gentlemen and had earned his B.A. in classics at Dalhousie University, he should accept with reluctance the logic of circumstances that sent all ambitious young men away from Nova Scotia.

> When I graduated from Dalhousie in the late nineteen-twenties I knew no other part of the world beyond the province and like most Nova Scotians I had no wish to leave home. . . . But I knew I would have to emigrate if I wanted to make a career and so did most of my classmates; it was something we all took for granted. (*TT*, 20)

MacLennan was more fortunate than most of his fellow graduates. In the year of 1929, when the world economic crisis closed the doors of opportunity for those who sought careers in the world outside, MacLennan won his Rhodes Scholarship and set out for Oxford. By the time he left Halifax he had paid his first visit to New York, but he had seen no other part of Canada than Nova Scotia and had felt no urge to do so.

At Oxford MacLennan entered Oriel College, and his first months there were curiously disturbed, not merely by the strangeness of English ways and the hard discipline of the Oxford tutorial system, but also—and here he showed his Celtic sensibility—by the very beauty of the ancient city, "so overwhelming that when I first en-

11

countered it I was lonely and unhappy for months, shaken as a man is when he encounters something almost too much for him" (SR, 193). Eventually he adjusted, made friends, acquired the blandness of manner and outlook distinguishing Rhodes Scholars from other Canadians, and became, as he has remained, something of a devotee of sports, exchanging the basketball he had played at Dalhousie for "a lovely game called rugger," and becoming a member of his college eleven. A more lasting attachment was to tennis, the game whose summer sounds echo through his books; he eventually became secretary of the Oxford University Lawn Tennis Club and played for Oxford against Cambridge.

I emphasise MacLennan's sporting activities because they represent an aspect of the man which has a great deal to do with his particular development as a novelist. He has never felt the need to withdraw from the world of ordinary affairs that is experienced by so many professional writers. To the contrary, as his later record shows, he found the purely literary life not merely unprofitable, but also mentally crippling when he tried it for six years between 1945 and 1951. He began as a scholar and, except for that brief period, he has always combined writing with the active existence of a teacher, and maintained his links with politicians and bureaucrats and business men as well as with the academy and with at least the purlieus of bohemia. Other Canadian writers have often looked askance at MacLennan's habit of lecturing to Canadian Clubs up and down the land, but, though this may indeed be a mark of conventionality, it is also a sign of the desire to understand and to assimilate mentally with ordinary unliterary people. This has helped Mac-

Lennan in creating the kind of novel—accessible to as well as representative of a wide range of Canadians—which he has chosen to write.

Oxford meant more to MacLennan than the acquisition of knowledge and a kind of *savoir faire*. He acquired an understanding of the English style which enabled him to respond with real empathy to that crucial moment in the decline of the empire, the Suez crisis of 1956, and to write about it in a fine threnody of an essay, "The Curtain Falls on the Grand Style," though he never made the mistake of imagining that a North American, even a Nova Scotian, could put back the clock of experience so far as to become an Englishman. Perhaps even more important, he spent every summer on the continent of Europe, where life was cheap as well as interesting. He travelled through France and Germany, through Switzerland and Italy; later he was to remark that before he crossed the New Brunswick frontier for the first time on his way to Montreal in 1935, he had seen most of the capitals of Europe.

In 1931 he went on the farthest journey, accompanying two of his Oxford friends on a walking trip to Greece, which they reached by ferry from Brindisi. They intended to study antiquities, and his companions did so, but MacLennan found himself moved more than historically by Greece. Those rocky landscapes he identified with Nova Scotia, as he likened the legendary past of Greece to that of his highland ancestors, and he sought to turn his feelings into poetry. Now, for the first time, he thought of becoming a writer. It was an unexpected transformation; until then, as he confessed, he had read little of English literature, and among that no novels, for since childhood he had concentrated on Greek and Latin.

But his ambitions quickly expanded; he began to think of writing plays, and then of writing novels.

In 1932 he left Oxford with a BA, adding an MA by the simple Oxonian way of paying an appropriate fee to the bursar of his college. Returning to Nova Scotia, he went to Dalhousie in search of a post. There was a single vacancy at Dalhousie in his field, but an Englishman was competing for it, and MacLennan was told by the head of the department that it was not even worth his time to apply; the Englishman would inevitably be preferred. He advised him to try the United States, where Canadians were supposed to be in demand. There, instead of a teaching post, MacLennan was glad to accept at Princeton in the autumn of 1932 a graduate fellowship that would assure him room and board, his tuition and nothing more.

The next three years he lived at Princeton in term time and spent the vacations touring every state north of the Mason-Dixon Line in an antiquated Studebaker which he had bought secondhand for a few dollars. He studied Roman History, and the subject of his Ph.D. thesis, *Oxyrhynchus,* was an Egyptian town that flourished beside the Nile and dwindled under Roman rule. Mac-Lennan set out to probe the disintegration in local government and the fraying of links with the imperial centre that led to a collapse of civil order and a general impoverishment of life in such peripheral communities as the Empire declined and decayed. In itself, the thesis now strikes one as an undistinguished example of routine historical scholarship, but it has an indirect interest for its bearing on the attitudes MacLennan carried over into his later writing.

The professional immersion in the classical past, which

was to continue another decade after he left Princeton in 1935, was to influence deeply the form and the symbolism of his novels. His later themes were determined largely by historical problems that preoccupied him at Princeton, for even then he saw in the decline of the Roman Empire and in the waning of the culture of cities that accompanied it, the "questions which somehow must be solved if our own culture is to survive" (O, 9); two at least of his novels, *Two Solitudes* and *Return of the Sphinx*, were to be profoundly concerned with this very question of the survival of a culture and the polity it inspired. Moreover, it must be noted that Oxyrhynchus was a *colonial* settlement which failed because it could develop no viable life of its own when the link with the imperial centre was broken; the resemblance between this situation and that of Canada as a colonial society moving into independence, with the perils that process incurred, must have been evident to MacLennan when he was writing his thesis, for a very short time afterwards the theme took its due place in his first published novel, *Barometer Rising*.

MacLennan's attention during those three years in the United States was increasingly occupied with the process of becoming a committed writer. During the summer of 1932, he had started to write a novel set in the United States. He completed it during his first year at Princeton, and it was accepted by a publisher who went bankrupt because of the depression, so that it was never published. MacLennan now talks of this piece of ill-luck as fortunate in the end; he realized afterwards that the novel was a literary failure, and today he is inclined to be reticent about it.

At Princeton MacLennan fell in with a group of young

15

Englishmen steeped in contemporary English and Continental writing. Under their guidance he read Eliot and Auden, Hemingway and Malraux, a novelist who mingled the social and the philosophical in highly dramatic forms and whom he admired greatly. He had already encountered the novels of Lawrence, whose influence, like most young writers of his generation, he undoubtedly felt, and now, "for two years I cramped my style by trying to write like James Joyce" (*SR*, 143), though it was probably the Joyce of *Dubliners* and *Portrait of the Artist as a Young Man* who held him temporarily captive rather than the Joyce of *Ulysses*, which he has confessed to finding hard to read to the end. Before he left Princeton he had, under these various influences, written a second novel, set in Europe. It never found a publisher, and it too MacLennan now dismisses as an apprentice work.

An important realization came to him in that period at Princeton.

> Steadily, during those first three years in the United States, the knowledge was borne in on me that I did not fit . . . A man needs a strange country to get a new sense of himself. But he needs his own country to be aware of his roots. Without using the phrase in the slightest sense nationalistically, I missed not being able to be a Canadian. (*CC*, 48-49)

So he returned to Halifax and found that his Ph.D. was useless in getting him a university post, as it was anywhere else in Canada. Eventually, in default of anything better, he accepted a job as schoolmaster, teaching Latin and history in Lower Canada College in Montreal. He stayed there for ten years.

The move to Montreal was decisive. "I emigrated and put down my roots in the continent and learnt to think in continental terms," and, though he could not forget "the poignancy with which I regarded Nova Scotia when I was young" (*TT*, 23), he began to think of himself as a Montrealer, and such he has remained ever since. He has travelled far over Canada and the United States; he has returned to Europe, visited his ancestral Highlands, seen the Scandinavian countries with their Canadian echoes and travelled in Russia during the Stalinist regime in 1937. But always he has returned to Montreal, and he has written copiously on the city, not only in three of his novels, but also in his essays, notably "Montrealer" (*SR*), "The St. Lawrence" (*7R*), and "City of Two Souls" (*TT*). He has freely evoked the look and atmosphere of the living city, has recorded and explained his love of it ("It is wonderful and utterly deplorable. It is magnificent and ridiculous . . . Few European cities can equal its tolerance or its wit" [*TT*, 64]), and has built upon it a city of the imagination which derives from the actual Montreal and from the lessons MacLennan has learnt there of the tensions and attractions that exist between what eventually he was to call, borrowing a pharse from Rilke, the "two solitudes" of Canada.

In Montreal, in those years when MacLennan was struggling to become a writer, he was swept along by the intellectual passions which he identifies with the idea of the Thirties. *The Watch that Ends the Night* was to become MacLennan's most substantial commentary on this era of his past, but all through his essays there are flashes of recollection that define the period. It was a generation "so angry that the modern youths who call themselves Angry Young Men seem by comparison like comfortable bourgeoisie," it was a generation riddled with "intellectual pride," it was a generation whose "psyches were tuned to meet total catastrophe."

Out of the intellectual furies of that time, and out of memories of childhood aroused in the congenial exile of Montreal, MacLennan wrote his first novel about Canada, which was also his first successful novel. It was *Barometer Rising* and it appeared in 1941. Immediately it established him as one of Canada's important younger writers, but it did not earn him enough money to live by his writing. With a break for a year in 1943, during which he lived in New York on a Guggenheim Fellowship, MacLennan remained at Lower Canada College until 1945. From then to 1951 he tried to live from a combination of book-writing, journalism and broadcasting; he became a regular participant in radio and later in television quiz shows. But he found that he could not support the insecurity which was the price of his freedom, and so in 1951 he returned to teaching, joining the faculty of McGill as a part-time lecturer in English and eventually in his late fifties rising to the position of a full professor.

With most writers it is the formative years that count biographically, for they shape essential attitudes and store the mind with the basic material of a life's work. Mac-Lennan has been no exception; after the publication of *Barometer Rising* his life tended to be governed mainly by the routines of writing and teaching, and the seasonal shift from his winter flat in Montreal to his summer home in the Eastern Townships. The novels followed each other at long intervals, for MacLennan is a slow writer who revises and rewrites copiously. *Two Solitudes* came in 1945,

The Precipice in 1948, and *Each Man's Son* in 1951; *The Watch That Ends the Night* appeared after a much longer interval in 1959, and *Return of the Sphinx*, again after eight years, in 1967. The volumes of essays have fitted into the intervals, as have the honours, five Governor-General's Awards (his worst book, *The Precipice* was crowned and two of his best, *Barometer Rising* and *Each Man's Son*, went capriciously unrewarded) and election to the Royal Society. The essays have accepted these routines, and have included little in the way of autobiographical detail about the later years, though they have said much that illuminates MacLennan's view of life and of his function as a writer in modern Canada.

III

WHERE A MAN STANDS

A writer's philosophic attitude is conditioned by the very fact that he is a writer, and also by the kind of writer he happens to be. For the plainly expository craftsman the problems involved in approaching the truth may be simple, since for him truth can have a single aspect. But the imaginative writer not only lives in a mental world of ambiguities, but the perception and the use of ambiguity are the conditions of his artistic success, since it is ambiguity that enlarges statement by suggestion, and extends the factual into the symbolic.

Hugh MacLennan is not a writer of great intricacy, and the tendencies towards naturalism and didacticism in his novels do not require the involutions of aesthetic philosophy which great experimental works demand and stimulate. Whatever MacLennan has written on his art and the philosophy that inspires it is couched in simple terms. Literary criticism has not attracted him, and he has rarely embarked upon it. Indeed, in his essays as in his life, he has preferred to appear rarely in the character of the artist and most characteristically in the role of the plain man seeking the good and fruitful life.

Even so, he is aware of the complexities which the simplest forms of imaginative writing involve (and his own, as we shall see, is by no means so simple as first reading might lead one to assume). There are many reasons, he realizes, why men write books. "One . . . is because we are lonely, and another is that we want to come to terms with our environment by telling the truth about it. These two desires are in painful conflict in any writer who has ever lived."

In that statement one fact becomes boldly evident: the idea of truth in relation to environment, which marks MacLennan as essentially a social novelist. Other truths— psychological truth, spiritual truth— are by no means excluded from his work, but essentially it is the truth about man as a social being, living with and among other men, that he is seeking out. To this extent he remains under the influence of the ideas about the social orientation of literature he acquired during the 1930's, even though that orientation in his case is not directed by a political philosophy of the left. Indeed, one of the lessons which MacLennan, like so many others, learnt from the Thirties was that a writer cannot afford to become a member of even the smallest of orthodoxies. He must stand on his own, and perhaps this is the first important element in MacLennan's philosophy of living.

In time one's profession, no matter what it is, teaches the inevitable lesson that a man must in final decisions be his own judge. Work must be for work's sake and nothing else. If one is to be unmoved by abuse, one must also be more or less unmoved by praise. In other words, one must choose between telling the truth and being liked. (*TT*, 250)

But truth is not all of a kind, and here the ambiguity enters in: "there are two kinds of truth for a writer:

emotional truth and the verity of judgment based on fact." Clearly, for MacLennan, the problem is to reveal both truths and to resolve the conflict that may lie between them.

In facing this problem MacLennan sees himself as the heir of a long humanistic tradition, a "continuum" of history whose last days came in the Thirties. For the true sense of the past as a soil in which one was rooted has withered among the youth of the post-war generation who are about to inherit the world. MacLennan became especially conscious of this fact after 1951, when he began teaching regularly at McGill. He encountered a generation which lived "in the shadow of no past older than 1945," a generation of youth unique in its lack of any sense of tradition whatever. "Nor will you be right if you pretend that you were just as oblivious to the past when you were their age. You weren't" (SR, 273).

World War II finally destroyed the continuum, but it had been breaking apart for a long time and MacLennan attributes the situation not to political and technological causes alone, but even more to the loss of faith and to the weakening of the humanist tradition which he attributes to the abandonment of the intellectual disciplines of a classical education. His description of what we have lost through the debasement of education merits quotation because it states by implication MacLennan's own view of the basis for a true and satisfying life.

The first loss, I should say, is the virtual disappearance of the old belief that life is a coherent experience.

The second loss—the result of the first—is of the

collective and individual self-confidence our fore-fathers knew, and which we ourselves knew for a brief while under Churchill's leadership in the last war.

The third loss—the result of the second—is the ancient respect for truth as something valuable and unassailable in itself, as something hard to find but precious, as something which cannot be juggled with by advertisers and politicians without regard to the final consequences, as something more important, however austere it may be, than conformity for the sake of comfort to any market-place necessity of the moment.

The fourth loss—the result of the third—is the old belief that education cannot be easy, that it does not lead to material security but to struggle, that at its best it is a pilgrim's progress to the heavenly city. (SR, 74-75)

In talking of "the heavenly city," as MacLennan makes very clear in this excellently argued essay ("The Classical Tradition and Education"), he does not intend a mere literary metaphor, for the first thing is to "get back to the primary business of education," which is to ask the questions that must be asked, even if they cannot be answered, if society is to survive: ". . . what is truth? What is the purpose of life? What is God's will?" (SR, 75). And here, though MacLennan expressed his willingness to use any synonym for "God" that might describe the intelligent force which inspires life and motion, we come to the essential core of his philosophic position: that he is a religious man, a man who carries a Bible in his suitcase and reads it, yet is in revolt against the Calvinist theology and the puritan ethics that darkened his childhood.

Thus, MacLennan rejects the secularist view that science has removed the necessity for religion. Science, he holds, has discredited an outdated theology. But theologies are only the temporary symbolic structures which churches have invented to try to convey in finite form some conception of an infinite being. The discrediting of the symbols does not destroy the truth they seek to express—the God who, in MacLennan's words, is "at once purpose and cause . . . the cause of our existence and the purpose behind the universe" (CC, 143). If science cannot prove the existence of God, that is due to science's own limitations.

> Yet it is only through mystical or poetic insight that man's ultimate experience—his relationship to the Universal Spirit—can be realized. Not all the exact knowledge in the world can substitute for the state of being which the wisdom of the centuries has affirmed to be the highest state to which the human spirit can rise. (CC, 156)

In fact, once limitations are recognized, science and mystical religion can live together, and there is no need for the sense of living in that "solitude of a purposeless universe," which is the theme of so much modern writing. It is, MacLennan declares, the puritan tradition that has made difficult the reconciliation of religion and science and has led into the impasse of agnosticism. It is obvious that MacLennan's detestation of puritanism is an intensely personal passion, which to an extent he exorcised by writing *Each Man's Son*.

24

Not merely has puritanism laid the burden of a cruel guilt upon those who are brought up under its shadow. It must also, in MacLennan's view, bear the responsibility for the growth of materialistic attitudes in the Protestant world, and for the retreat from spiritual values. In other words, puritanism is—if we accept MacLennan's arguments—to be taken as an anti-religion.

Religion can never be anything save a thing of the spirit: its values are of the spirit, its aims are of the spirit. But the society in which we live has become so materialistic that even our standards of goodness are in general materialistic ones. It is not a change in our judgment of what constitutes evil that marks the extent of our drift from our spiritual past. It is the change in our judgment of what is good.

In the past, a man's goodness was primarily measured by his devotion to God, by his service to God, and neither of these phrases then seemed mysterious or obscure. Today a man's goodness is measured—at least in the non-Catholic world—by his material services to his fellow men. (CC, 140)

In the essay from which this quotation comes, "Help Thou Mine Unbelief," he goes on to stress that no matter how much material goodness there may be in a society, it cannot indefinitely continue to be religious without a strong spiritual element. It can remain Christian in the sense that the ethic expounded in the New Testament still inspires its life; MacLennan agrees that people who have lost all faith may still live in the twilight of Christ's teaching as gentle and considerate people. But, as history

25

shows, "no civilization has long survived after that civilization has lost its religion" (*CC*, 140). Though MacLennan does not put it in such archaic terms, he clearly means that the loss of spirituality in a culture means the coming of anti-Christ, for, as he says, "where religion is concerned nature abhors a vacuum," and that vacuum—in our age—is likely to be filled by movements like Nationalism, Fascism and Communism, which he quite correctly argues "are fundamentally neither political not economic movements. They are, in their appeal to the masses and even to intellectuals, aberrations of the religious impulse" (*CC*, 141).

I have dwelt at some length on MacLennan's views on religion in our age, because these have a clearer relevance than has been recognized by most to the content and even the actual form and symbolism of his novels. The solutions he sketches out are, of necessity, vague and tentative, since the mystical insight is not something one can create to order, nor is the confidence in an immanent spiritual order which has inspired so many societies in their greatest period. One can only talk of such things in symbols, and, as MacLennan points out, the symbols that once were significant have lost their magic, largely because puritanism has appropriated the concept of the "practical Jesus," and has lost the vision of God. What is needed—and MacLennan confesses by implication that he has not found it—is "a new way to express the idea of God" (*CC*, 148).

It is small wonder that a man so disturbed about the spiritual condition of the world should at times look back so nostalgically on a Victorian past, the past when it was possible to live like the old Nova Scotian captain, Joshua Slocum. Slocum's book, *Sailing Around the World* (the record of a one-man voyage in a nine-ton boat), formed the subject of one of MacLennan's few essays that might be called a book review ("An Easy Mind"). Slocum was a *secure* man, secure "in his courage and skill, his faith in God," and this was what aroused MacLennan's admiration.

> Too many of our most admired living authors write as though fear were more interesting than courage and lust more fascinating than love. In a world of waste and propaganda, where the young lions are naked and dead from here to eternity, Joshua Slocum's brave happiness shines like the beam of a lighthouse across the cold, dark water of our fears. (*TT*, 261)

We shall see MacLennan trying to capture the now elusive beam of that old lighthouse of spiritual happiness in book after book, and perhaps, in a literary sense, the most important aspect of MacLennan's religious views will be the way in which they mark him off—as his techniques do in another way—as a writer emphatically, but not necessarily fatally, out of period and fashion. Without pretending to be in any way religiously inspired, admitting his unwilling lack of the power to give living expression to the idea of God, he refuses to accept the pessimism that has marked a great spectrum of modern literature, ranging from the defiant heroism before the absurd postulated by Malraux and Camus to the acceptance of what appears to be a total lack of meaning in human life by

27

writers like Beckett and Robbe-Grillet. Rather he turns in admiration to a group of un-named writers whom he mentions in his essay. "The Future of the Novel as an Art Form," the producers of what he calls "strong novels," whose essential attitude to life he expresses in terms which strike one as delineating accurately his own attitude to life and to the ways in which a novelist should portray it.

> Invariably they have been books dealing with real people in situations in which the cards were not stacked arbitrarily against them. Some were even books which accepted as a living force an entity dismissed with derision in the Twenties and Thirties. That entity is the mystery the Stoics called the World Soul and Christians and Jews call God. Some novels have even presented decent people as interesting and competent. (SR, 156)

Decent people! The phrase arouses what at first seems an incongruous echo. For George Orwell was of course the writer in our time who was constantly talking about the virtues of decency, and at first it seems difficult to find much in common between MacLennan and that relentless satirist and radical. Yet in a way they were two sides of the same coin. In both there is the nostalgia for a more secure and more meaningful way of life that has somehow been lost in the past; in both there is a disgust with the values of the present. If MacLennan appears the more conservative, it is perhaps only because we have not quite recognized how much of Orwell's radicalism was in fact Tory radicalism. Yet MacLennan is inclined to take far more on trust than Orwell; he never shows the urge that Orwell felt to strip aside the layers of pretended decency and to reveal the sham which he saw everywhere in human relations as they exist in the modern world.

There are some ways, of course, in which MacLennan seems the epitome of the conservative mind, almost a throwback to the tweedy English novelists of Georgian days in his preoccupation with his country house and his tree-felling and his roses and his tennis, in his ability to write well in the almost obsolete form of the familiar essay, in his feeling (which I confess to sharing) that there is no music as good as that of the Baroque age.

Yet he is capable of taking his romantic nostalgias firmly in hand on occasion, of pointing out that the age of Haydn was also the age of Captain Bligh, and that the perfection of music and of the polite life which glorified the times of Mozart and Bach and Haydn was accompanied by a lapse or perhaps rather an absence of conscience.

Here, it seems to me, MacLennan brings himself to the brink of a rather horrifying dilemma. For he declares that our twentieth century differs from the eighteenth in being an age of conscience. "For all its horrors, the twentieth century is better than the eighteenth; no politician or dictator who has tried to defy its conscience has been able, in the end, to succeed" (*TT*, 152). Perhaps . . . though one may doubt whether all those who defy the conscience of our age have failed (Stalinism is a remarkably tough growth), and one may also say that in the end the Blighs too were failures, since the nineteenth century changed the rules of the game in their disfavour. However, those historical doubts are perhaps less important in the context

29

than MacLennan's linking of the diminution of the arts in our age with the development of a sensitive conscience. "For a conscience, as Shakespeare knew when he created Hamlet, inhibits action and beclouds genius. Our collective conscience may not have made the modern artist a coward, but it has certainly made him a prisoner" (*TT*, 150).

If we think at this point of MacLennan's statements about the effects of puritanism in the weakening of the spiritual life, we come to an interesting syllogism on the basis of the essay I have just quoted, "The Shadow of Captain Bligh." 1. The present, becoming less spiritual, has become more moral. 2. In becoming more moral, it has become less inspired in the arts. 3. Thus a Christian morality, lived out, seems incompatible with both the spiritual and the artistic lives. I do not believe this, and I doubt if, on closer consideration, MacLennan does.

Certainly if these arguments prove nothing else, they show that MacLennan is not a very clear thinker or a very consistent man. In a novelist these are not necessarily disqualifications, especially when, as will become evident in his case, that novelist relies more than at first seems apparent in his writing on the movements of the unconscious mind.

IV

A NATION'S AWAKENING

In his evident and directly expressed concern for the growth and unity of Canada, and for the self-realization of Canadians, Hugh MacLennan appears as a Canadian novelist but he is not a political novelist in the sense of advocating or projecting any particular political doctrine or programme. What concerns him, in a rather strict and classical way, is the *polis*, the community of men and women, and children as well, gathered together into a political structure which, for MacLennan, is the nation. The nation, of course, is not the same as the land, for, as MacLennan insists, Canada is

> . . . a land larger than any one person can hope to comprehend, but containing what is still only a very small nation. The land, of course, will last as long as the world does, but the nation is only a tenant on it. (CO, 8)

Even in thinking of MacLennan's political attitude in national terms, it is necessary to remember the reservations on the subject of nationalism that are made in his essays. He is fully aware of the difference between moral man and the amoral nation, and there is one essay, "Help Thou Mine Unbelief" (CC), in which he sees this dichotomy as containing "the essence of our modern dilemma." The passage in which he discusses this question is almost necessary reading before we proceed to the view of Canada that inspires and permeates MacLennan's writing.

> . . . As individuals we lead on the whole kindly lives. But as nations we are proud, cruel, wanton, vindictive and more often than not destructive.
>
> Individual decency stems largely from our acceptance of much of Christ's ethics in our daily lives. National wickedness derives from our loss—in some cases total—of the idea of a divine providence.
>
> Mankind, having lost his nearness to the traditional God of the Christian religion, having come more and more to think of Christ as merely the most perfect human being who ever lived, has for over a century been striving frantically to recreate the God idea he has lost in the shape of a national state. It is our tragedy that this effort has been largely successful.
>
> A great national state, no matter what its pretensions, rests fundamentally on power and on nothing else. At best it stands for the order of the policeman, as Rome, Britain and the United States have stood or now stand for order. (CC, 142)

There seems indeed to be a marked ambivalence in MacLennan's attitude towards the nation, just as in his attitude towards power itself. In his novels men obsessed with power appear generally as negative figures, but in one of the most curious of his essays, a celebration of the photographer Yousuf Karsh, he dwells with fascination upon the faces of British and American leaders who in World War II generated the kind of ruthless power that ensured the destruction of the Nazis. There is a touch of naive wonder, almost of *schwärmerei*, in the way he regards their cold and distant expressions, the controlled brutality of their features. Yet, however uneasily he may view the inhumanity of the national state, he is certainly no anarchist: in the last resort he accepts the very basic fact of the survival of the state—that "somebody must assume the burden of power if organized society is to exist" (CC, 73). He regards it literally as a burden, since he sees the man of power condemned to loneliness, to starvation of the spirit, to the use of evil against evil, and in the last and most dreadful resort to committing the paradox of guarding civilization by acting like a savage.

The very nature of MacLennan's novels has made him an observer of the man of power in action, and especially of the national leader in the modern world. Churchill he has admired greatly, as a restorer of the world, as the man who grappled with the death wish that had seized the people of his time and, like a modern Heracles, destroyed it. Acting as observer for a Canadian magazine at the Republican Congress in 1948, when Dewey was selected as candidate, he had an extraordinary opportunity of watching the strange rituals of American leader-making and he made an illuminating comment on the character of national leadership.

> Great national leaders, especially within a democracy, are usually one of three different species of men. One kind, the most colourless, is the pure administrator. Another kind, always the most beloved, is a national replica of the father-image which resides within us all. The third kind, the most dangerous of all, is the symbol of youth in revolt. (CC, 113)

33

These words were written more than twenty years ago, and, read today, they demonstrate a penetrating—or perhaps merely a lucky—foresight into the political perils that have clearly emerged from the youth revolt of the later 1960's, a revolt that MacLennan has observed with misgivings, and has woven into the substance of his most recent novel, *Return of the Sphinx*.

Yet, whatever reservations he may have about the negative aspects of nationalism, or the amoralism of the men who wield power, there is no doubt of the presence in MacLennan's novels of a strong but benign form of nationalism. Indeed, he is the first novelist in the history of his country who has been able to take the drama of the development and survival of Canada and to use it effectively as the framework for fiction. This nationalism which irradiates the novels is compounded of a deep love of the physical land and a sense of belonging to a group of peoples which, despite geographical anomalies and historic divisions, has plunged into the primeval wilderness the roots of a unique human community.

In *Seven Rivers of Canada* and in the centennial picture book for which he wrote the text, *The Colour of Canada*, MacLennan's love of the land is declared most emphatically and explicitly, especially when he records his journeys down the Red and the Mackenzie Rivers to their wild and deserted northern deltas. The Mackenzie gave him not only the deepest feeling of the sheer physical vastness of Canada, but also a sense of how the land preserved its own life, enclosing the human community, exploited by it, and yet in its own way free from it.

In a moment of panic—the noun is accurately

chosen—I wondered if human beings are necessary on this earth. Here was this colossal land, here this wild beauty, here this huge inland sea to the south feeding the great river that poured for twelve hundred miles through the wilderness to the world's most useless ocean, above the Antarctic. What did the Creator want it all for? (7R, 53)

Yet at the same time, as he sailed and drove beside the great rivers, gathering the material for his book, Mac-Lennan felt his sense of Canadian history, and even of his own place in it, slowly becoming complete. For it was the rivers, and the men who travelled by them a century and a half ago, that made possible the greater Canada we know today; "without the rivers, the early nation could never have survived. The plains and British Columbia would have been fatally severed from the older communities of the Canadian east" (7R, 4). And so when MacLennan travelled by the Saskatchewan and the Mackenzie and the Fraser (for some unexplained reason he neglected those other great fur trading rivers, the Thompson and the Columbia) he felt that he had almost a personal stake in the great west which his own people had done so much to explore and to claim as British and eventually Canadian soil. Those who came on to the west instead of being content to put down roots in Cape Breton or in the more westerly Highland settlements like Glengarry in Ontario, were impelled by their desire for freedom and, as MacLennan remarks, the price of freedom in early Canada was "hardship and endurance." The triumph over the hardships at times produced greatness;

Alexander Mackenzie, in MacLennan's eyes, was "a giant among our people" (7R, 58).

As for the actual crystallization of the Canadian nation after the Highland fur traders and their French Canadian *voyageurs* had explored the west, MacLennan has no doubt that it was brought into being through an outside and accidental influence which acted as a catalyst; "without meaning to do so, the United States brought about the establishment of a nation composed of people who had no desire to unite" (CC, 15). The time came for people who called themselves North American, when a choice had to be made between submitting to the continental march of Manifest Destiny and deciding to become a nation on their own; "it was because Canadians had no wish to alienate themselves from the past and from their European source that the Canadian nation came into being" (7R, 15).

The idea that Canada is "not a logical construction" fascinates MacLennan; he seems to regard this illogical, improvised quality as something essential to Canada's survival, distinguishing it from the United States with its elaborately contrived mechanism of government, and giving it some of the tenacity of a natural growth.

Canadian social history MacLennan sees as a steady regression from the hardship and the toughness of the pioneer days. "Step by step in the nineteenth century, leap by leap in the twentieth, Canadian society has fled from its past." Overshadowing MacLennan's view of that progression, two great symbolic personalities preside in somewhat incongruous juxtaposition: Sir John A. Macdonald and Mackenzie King.

There is no doubt that MacLennan's Highland ancestry

emerges very emphatically when he chooses his Canadian heroes. Sir Alexander Mackenzie was born in Stornoway. Sir John A. Macdonald, though born in Glasgow, was Highland to his devious core. Mackenzie King is not, for MacLennan, a hero; a mere quarter Mackenzie, he is—or for a long time was—an obsession.

In his eulogies of Sir John, MacLennan displays an uncharacteristic lack of restraint. Macdonald is not only "our greatest citizen"; he is also among "the three or four supreme statesmen of the entire nineteenth century," the "one indispensable man" in the creation of the Commonwealth, while, according to MacLennan, "it is not easy to dig out of nineteenth century history the peer of the first prime minister of Canada." (*SR*, 105-9). There is more in an even more elevated and lyrical vein about Sir John, and we are left wondering about this fiery enthusiasm for Old Tomorrow. Such enthusiasm can only be explained by the loyalty one Highland Celt strikes in another, and perhaps also in part by the thought that if Canada is an illogical, improvised and therefore flexible political entity, Sir John was the eccentric mechanic who presided over its putting together.

In spite of Macdonald's efforts, Canada—as MacLennan admits—was for years hardly more than a collection of disunited provinces linked, after a while, by the thin thread of a railway. The Maritimes, the two Canadas, were separate settled societies, and out in the west a new society was growing where, as MacLennan sees it, for the first time the idea of Canada began to take living shape, almost as a necessary consequence of the terrain.

A Nova Scotian can still feel at home in his local

37

county, a French Canadian in a parish along the river, an Ontario man in a small town beside the lake. But countries and localities mean little on the ocean-like plain between St. Boniface and the Rockies, and out there people think in larger geographical horizons if not in larger human terms. Canada herself—that was the Westerner's notion of home! And during the last thirty years this western attitude has been growing to the proportions of a new force in Canadian politics. (SR, 267)

Not until the 1950's did the western vision take its full place in Canadian politics when the hour called out of obscurity the strange figure of John Diefenbaker. MacLennan met him on the morrow of his 1958 election victory, and remembered that he had encountered him twice before, and had been unimpressed. But this time it seemed that he had never before met "a Canadian public figure with such messianic passion." A "volcanic force" had been unleashed, and MacLennan suspected that what freed it was "the sense of vindication which comes to a man advanced in years who at last discovers a public willing to accept what he has been offering all his life" (SR, 269).

War and Peace is the novel and Tolstoy the novelist whom MacLennan admires most of all, and there is much of Tolstoy's idea of history making men great by choosing them as its instruments in MacLennan's view of the development of Canada. He saw Diefenbaker as a man made great by his time, and the circumstances of that time, in MacLennan's view, were the national revulsion against the knowledge that the Liberals, dominated by the American-reared C. D. Howe and the businessmen of the Laurentian region, had failed to protect Canada against the economic power of the United States. The result was a genuine political upheaval, the first in Canadian history.

> Too many people have endured too much—too many people have hoped too much—for this strange, illogical Canadian adventure to perish, or for this outbroken spirit to be processed into something with no more soul than a business corporation. After nearly two centuries of blind groping, the image of a Canadian identity has finally emerged out of the shell, and it is too late to push it back again. This force which Mr. Diefenbaker has tapped may be intangible, but it is a very real one indeed, and its political assertion is revolutionary in the most exact sense of the word. (SR, 271)

For twenty years before the Diefenbaker revolution, MacLennan, with considerable prophetic insight, had been charting in his novels the process of blind groping—and sometimes intelligent effort—through which "the image of a Canadian identity" had emerged. His first three novels, *Barometer Rising*, *Two Solitudes* and *The Precipice*, in one way or another, are dominated by this search, and the process by which he sees the sense of identity—the conception of Canada as a living and viable and individual community—emerging can be traced in the successive volumes of essays.

In MacLennan's boyhood, Canada was stunned by its losses in the First World War and hardly stirred out of its sleep of exhaustion—except in provincial spasms of discontent, for on the peripheries and especially in the Maritimes the total economic and political control wielded from Ottawa by men obsessed by the financial possibilities of the prairies, was deeply resented. "Bitterness and frustration were the fruits we ate from Confederation" (*TT*, 18).

In the days of Mackenzie King, "We were, and yet we were not, a nation." King's bizarre personality, with all its carefully concealed complexities, personified Canada's mood in the years when the depression faded into World War II.

> His genius for compromise, his massive public hypocrisy balanced by his uncanny personal acumen, his humourlessly drab style, his capacity to turn his incapacity for leadership into a political asset, the psychological conjuring act which enabled him to live in two worlds at once (Ottawa and the hereafter)—in the days of the Liberal glory, Mackenzie King could almost be called the outward and visible expression of the nation's subconscious mind. (*SR*, 263-4)

In that subconscious mind (note the collective mystique that is very strong in all MacLennan's writings about Canada and especially in his novels) Canadians were beginning to find themselves as "a people awakening at last to their strength and a new vision of their country's beauties" (*CC*, 19); "regardless of our origins or of the language we might happen to speak" we yearned "for a true national home in which at least we would be our own masters" (*TT*, 230).

Like the creation of Canada at Confederation, Mac-Lennan attributes this strengthening of national feeling to the catalytic presence of the United States, this time as an economic rather than a political threat. His attitude to America has always been complex, a mingling of respect and fear. He has lived and travelled in the United States, has married an American wife, and obviously feels a great deal of affection for the American land and the American people. Yet he returned gladly to Canada after his years at Princeton, and when he spent a winter in California for his wife's health, he fled back to Montreal with the first touch of spring and never repeated the experiment.

Apart from his emotional involvement with the Canadian people, MacLennan considers Canada a better place politically than the United States. The Canadian governmental system he sees as more flexible than the American, and for this reason he believes Canadians enjoy a truer democracy. Canada is also less prone to the North American plague of uniformity than its southern neighbour:

> The United States wiped out the European past of its citizens. But Canada seems to encourage all of us to remember where we came from in Europe. (CC, 44)

The relationship between Canada and the United States, while it is blessed on one side by the great knowledge Canadians have of their neighbours' country and its affairs, is bedevilled on the other by the almost complete ignorance among Americans regarding Canada, a grievance to which MacLennan often returns. But the central point of Canadian-American relations in this era, he believes, will inevitably be "the saving of Canada from the maw of American corporations," the battle against American domination.

The one great reason why Canada is unlikely to succumb to the uniformity that has overtaken the United States is, in MacLennan's view, the presence of "the Province of Quebec in its heart" (CC, 56). The relations between French and English speaking Canadians dominate what is probably MacLennan's most-read novel, *Two Solitudes*, which has made the title phrase from Rilke into a Canadian cliché. In *Return of the Sphinx* the problem re-emerges in more acute form. This deep fictional concern with the relations between the two principal Canadian peoples compares with a much shallower treatment of the problem in the essays, and this is perhaps the most striking illustration of the divergence between the rational and generally optimistic MacLennan of the discursive and expository writings, and the other self, so greatly moved by intuition, so sensitive to collective impulses, so much more inclined to pessimism, who finds expression in his novels.

Essentially, what strikes one when MacLennan talks of the French Canadian question in his essays is his desire to prove in one way or another that the division is a dynamic tension between two spheres that will never fly apart. In "The Canadian Chracter," an essay written in 1949, he remarks of Mackenzie King:

He knew that no matter how deep lie the emotions of the people, no matter how profound their frustrations, French and English alike have an overriding common aim upon which the Canadian national character, whatever its individual manifestations may be, firmly rests. Both groups know subconsciously that the security their ancestors lost so dramatically, and which their descendants so painfully regained, must be preserved at any price. (*CC*, 16-17)

Five years later, in 1954, he admires the way the two peoples of Montreal live together, each conscious of its superiority over the other, and both avoiding trouble by "building the barriers higher still," yet in 1961, in *Seven Rivers of Canada,* while emphasizing the same complex of barriers, he nevertheless sees a "collective pattern" in which the inhabitants of the two original Canadas come together as "the Laurentian people," inhabiting Ontario and Quebec and sharing interests and attributes they do not share with other Canadians. In his essays the picture is almost as serene as the prose is urbane. In the novels it is darkened and disturbed.

Indeed, sensible though MacLennan's essays may be in their argument, pleasing as they may be in their tone and balance, one ends reading them with the feeling that, like eighteenth century landscaping, they are designed to tame and arrange reality rather than to reveal it. Apart from their intrinsic interest as comprising almost half the writing MacLennan has thought fit to preserve in bound form, they provide a mass of information about the author and his interests and occupations (though rarely about his deep and intimate feelings). Yet one is always aware of their other function, as the mask which conceals the face the author does not choose to reveal. For, while one is conscious of being in the company of a civilized and almost Augustan mind, while one listens to the pleasant monologue spoken in a bland and level voice, one never pictures a living, visible personality as one does in such a small masterpiece of imaginative autobiography as Morley Callaghan's *That Summer in Paris*.

The fact is, one always feels nearer to reality in Mac-Lennan's fiction than in anything else he writes, and that is surely a good point from which to view the other, more important half of his work, the work of the novelist.

V

THE ART AND CRAFT OF FICTION

If Hugh MacLennan is concerned almost to the point of obsession with the development of a Canadian nation and of a sense of national identity among its people, he is equally convinced of his own historic role in that development, and in this he is undoubtedly right.

His sense of his own position is related to his view of the development of literature in Canada. His theory is that, except for the epic genre, a literature can only appear in a society reaching maturity; indeed, its emergence is one of the signs of that condition having been attained. He compares the Canadian experience with the American. A century and a half after the Pilgrim Fathers, the writings of Benjamin Franklin heralded the appearance of a literature that was no longer merely colonial but identifiably American. A century and a half after the arrival of the Loyalists marked the birth of English Canada, we reach the depression years, the hungry and angry Thirties, and MacLennan fixes 1940 as the approximate date when "a Canadian public was willing to accept a specifically Canadian city as a credible and interesting setting for a novel" (SR, 140).

One can argue about the exact date. F. R. Scott, E. J. Pratt and Frederick Philip Grove were all creating prior to 1940 works of verse and prose which were characteristically Canadian. But a difference of a few years in the dating is unimportant. Canada did begin to reach social and political maturity towards the end of the depression and its first indigenous literary flowering began at the same time. By 1939 MacLennan was ready to write his first novel, *Barometer Rising,* and this was also—as he points out—the first novel about a *specifically* Canadian city, as distinguished from the use of Canadian settings in a vague and generalized way of novelists—like Morley Callaghan—writing in Canada before him.

Here, undoubtedly, lies MacLennan's claim to be a pioneering and original novelist—the reason why, as Hugo McPherson has said, *"Barometer Rising* marks a major advance in Canadian fiction." MacLennan was the first writer to realize and to express in a form that would be widely acceptable the social realities of Canada in the mid-twentieth century.

He has told how he came to accept that mission. He had written a novel set in the United States and another set in Europe, and after the accidents that prevented both of them from being published, he reached the conclusion that he must write a new kind of Canadian novel that would not only characterize Canada but would also escape the limitations of mere regionalism. It must therefore be directed at two audiences.

One was the Canadian public, which took the Canadian scene for granted but had never defined its particular essence. The other was the international public, which had never thought about Canada at all, and knew nothing whatever about us. (*TT,* 51-2)

46

In practice, MacLennan has always tried to write for readers outside as well as within Canada, and, while he has attracted relatively little attention in Britain, his novels have sold well in the United States and have gained approval from such establishment critics as Edmund Wilson.

There is no doubt that in this role of the interpretive social novelist MacLennan found a genre suited to his discursive talents as a writer. One can best accept him as an example of the kind of novelist that may be necessary in Canada today, the kind of novelist who interprets a rapidly expanding society to its own people in the same way as Dickens and Balzac interpreted the society of the industrial revolution to the English and French a century before. MacLennan obviously has not the variety or the abounding vigour or the sheer greatness of texture shared by these imperfect giants, yet in his own way he shares their role, and no other writer has yet come nearer than he to writing a Canadian *Comédie Humaine*.

It is the implications of this role that MacLennan sees most clearly when he considers—as he has frequently done—his career as a novelist. The Canadian novelist, he claims, is bound to be concerned as much with the effect of environment on his characters as he is with their personal idiosyncracies. Such, he tells us in the essay "Where is My Potted Palm?" (*TT*) were the thoughts that filled his mind when he was about to start work on *Barometer Rising*.

> He must describe, and if necessary define, the social values which dominate the Canadian scene, and do so in such a way as to make them appear interesting

and important to foreigners. Whether he liked it or
not, he must for a time be something of a geographer,
a historian and a sociologist, to weave a certain
amount of geography, history and sociology into his
novels. Unless he did so, his stories would be set in
a vacuum. He could not, as British and American
writers do, take his background values for granted,
for the simple reason that the reading public had no
notion what they were. He must therefore do more
than write dramas, he must also design and equip
the stage on which they were to be played. (*TT*,
52)

The didactic urge, and the topographical and documentary tasks which MacLennan accepts, have inclined
him towards a type of fiction which aims at verisimilitude
within the framework of a socio-political vision. Combined
with his rejection of the image of the writer as a being
detached from the society in which he lives, and with his
consciousness that "literature . . . must grow out of society
itself" (*SR*, 137), these necessities have led MacLennan
to adopt a style that combines elements of romanticism
and popular realism. Reading his novels, one is at first
impressed by their relative conservatism in form and
technique; Edmund Wilson even found points of resemblance to Sir Walter Scott. Apart from the didacticism
which in more sophisticated literary traditions would appear irremediably old-fashioned, they rely much more
heavily than most modern fiction on environmental atmosphere and local colour; their characterization is over-
simplified and moralistic in tone; their language is descriptive rather than evocative; and their action tends to be

48

shaped externally by an almost Hardyesque combination of circumstance and coincidence. MacLennan found in the tradition of the realist novel the means to present his vision, and nothing he has written can in a stylistic sense be regarded as experimental. He claims, it is true, to have discovered in the writing of *The Watch that Ends the Night* "new techniques I had previously known nothing about" ("The Story of a Novel," *Canadian Literature* 3, Winter 1960), but nobody on examining the novel has been quite sure what he meant by this statement, since even this most ambitious of his works, with its bold flash-backs, uses no structural or stylistic device that has not been in common use by writers for the past forty or fifty years.

Indeed, it is obvious from the way MacLennan discusses his own books that he is not the kind of writer who has a deeply theoretical approach to his work. When he talks of his career as a writer and also of the general role of the novel, he is preoccupied with issues that have little directly to do with the creative process or the novels it produces. In "The Story of a Novel" he talks about his books almost as if they were commodities, discussing the financial returns from them, and relating these to the actual quantity of work each has involved in terms of words written and used or discarded. In a series of curious calculations he reveals such staggering facts as that to reach the 100,000 words of *Barometer Rising* he wrote 700,000 words, and that the 140,000 words of the final version of *The Watch that Ends the Night* probably involved a total of more than 3 million words of writing! As such figures show, MacLennan is the kind of writer who is not only slow at producing a novel, but proceeds by the method of cutting his final version out of a vast out-pouring of words.

MacLennan's inclination to view his work at times in commodity terms is related quite closely to his view of the relationship between the writer and the reader, which is discussed at great length in "The Future of the Novel as an Art Form" (SR). There MacLennan lays a particular stress on the "true-to-life" aspect of fiction. The virtue of a novel lies for him in its power to "make social situations live" and to "clothe political and economic forces with flesh and blood." This, one would assume, rules out from legitimacy in MacLennan's eyes the novel considered as fantasy. Indeed, he specifically deplores what he regards as "one of the most curious aspects of the revolution in literature . . . the discarding of the age-old axiom that unless a book or a poem is a communication, it does not really exist."

He clearly does not discard the axiom. He states, on the contrary, that "no writer can indefinitely get away with it if he despises the public, nor can any writer hold the public if he consistently distorts truth." The true public of the novel he regards as the people generally described as middle-brow, "the serious reader who knows himself to be an individual and is also a responsible citizen compe-tent to earn a living, raise a family and even to vote."

For the good father, good citizen, and fundamentally good man who is this ideal reader, MacLennan envis-ages a kind of novel which will concentrate on such solidly old-fashioned things as well-realized characters, complexity of plot, strength of "story-line"; in other words, the kind of novel he himself writes. Novels can be satis-fying only if they go beyond merely expressing the personalities of their writers, and "do certain things for their readers." These "certain things" MacLennan describes thus.

> First, the satisfying novel must entertain them; it must so grip them that when they enter the book they cannot be easy until they have finished it. Then it must make the reader a part of the world of the novelist's creation, and this it does by creating fictional characters more real than the reader's personal friends. In order to make characters like these, the novelist must also create the backgrounds and locales in which the characters move, and make them consistent and vivid. A satisfying novel must also hold all of its descriptions, dialogues, ideas, arguments, scenes and actions, within a whole which is harmonious, within a whole where the surprises are seen in retrospect to have been inevitable. And in the supremely satisfying novels, as in all good works of art, there is finally a mystery. (SR, 146-7)

In another essay MacLennan says of great books that they have in common "a haze of ambiguity which makes it difficult . . . for readers to know just how true they are," and that when we read such books "we seem to sink down through various layers of thought and feeling until we are in danger of losing ourselves." It is the ambiguity and the unexpected layers of thought and feeling in MacLennan's books that, if they do not make them great, at least make them much more than ordinary romantic-idealist novels intended for well-meaning members of the Book-of-the-Month Club. If academic critics and other writers as well as middlebrow readers take MacLennan very seriously, it is because there is much more in his books than meets the immediate eye, in the sense of patterns of imagery and symbolism supporting a structure of universal myth whose presence is due to the movements of an active unconscious beneath the deliberate and didactic intent which gives a general shape to his novels.

I became aware of the astonishing part the unconscious plays in MacLennan's writing when I pointed out ("A Nation's Odyssey," *Canadian Literature*, 10, Autumn 1961) that the great unifying myth of his novels was the *Odyssey* translated into terms of modern life. I pointed out that the *Odyssey* was the product of a people in the process of becoming aware of itself, and that MacLennan had appropriately used the myth to illuminate the growth of a Canadian national consciousness. This analysis, which has generally been accepted by other critics, was supported not only by patterns of action and personal relationship recurring from novel to novel, but also by clues so specific that it seemed to me at the time that the choice of the *Odyssey* as a prototype could not be other than deliberate, particularly in view of the fact that in several essays MacLennan had referred to his childhood fascination with the poem. For example:

When I was a boy, I read Homer, first in abridged translations for children, later in the original. Although the *Iliad* was composed about a millenium before Christ and the *Odyssey* perhaps a hundred and fifty years later, both books seemed to me to be almost contemporary. True, the Cape Breton miners on pay nights did not fight with spears . . . But it required no effort of the imagination . . . to think myself into the atmosphere of Homer. It was all around me in Nova Scotia when I was young. (*TT*, 13)

This memory stayed with him so vividly that it not only found its way into his essays, but was transferred to at least one of his characters; Paul Tallard, in *Two Solitudes*.

In view of so many indications of the centrality of the *Odyssey* in Hugh MacLennan's literary universe, I was astonished to receive a letter from him in which he expressed his surprise at the parallel I had suggested, though he did not deny its validity. I quote from his letter, which was published more fully in *Canadian Literature* (No 13, Summer 1962):

Until I read your essay, it had never consciously occurred to me that I was following the Odyssey-myth in these books. The choice of the name Penelope in *Barometer Rising* may have been subconsciously prompted, but the passage at the end where it seemed most obvious that I was rubbing the symbol in was not much more than a device, and rather a corny one at that, used by an inexperienced author to conclude his book. As for the others, it never once occurred to me consciously that the events were paralleling the *Odyssey*, least of all the smash-up scene at the end of *Each Man's Son*. I was bothered by the Enoch Arden aspect of Martell in the last novel, but it never occurred to me that once again this was Odysseus returning.

It is this self-admitted factor of the unconscious that has not only provided MacLennan with a central myth that relates Canadian experiences with uncanny accuracy to a universal condition; it is also the explanation for the unexpected layers of meaning we encounter in all the books. As the reader will observe, I have not abandoned my contention that the recognition of the presence and significance of the Odysseus myth as a guiding structure is central to the understanding of MacLennan's novels.

VI

THE DOUBLE EXPLOSION

The setting of MacLennan's first novel, *Barometer Rising,* is Halifax during the First World War. The novel opens when a young man comes back secretly to the Nova Scotian capital; enough is revealed in the first pages to suggest that there is a mystery involved in his coming, and then, immediately, we are plunged in a long description of the city as seen through the eyes of this exile who returns; the town, we realize, will play as great a part in the novel as any of the merely human characters.

The action is contained within what is almost a unity of time—it takes place in a total of eight days—and within a unity of place (Halifax and its environs) which, except for flashbacks in the minds of the characters, is complete. The resemblance to the classical Greek drama which MacLennan knew so well is increased by the fact that, as Hugh McPherson has pointed out, "we are to be present only at the climacteric events." Indeed, it is only one really climacteric event in which we do participate as direct observers—the great explosion that destroys half of Halifax and precipitates so many of the decisions within the novel. Other events that have a great bearing on the fates of the main characters take place—again as in Greek drama—off stage, and we hear of them only through the conversation of the characters, or in their memories, or through evidence presented to us after the event.

Barometer Rising is probably the most neatly planned and the most classical in its outline of all MacLennan's novels, and MacLennan certainly never surpassed the felicity with which, in this third book (if we count the two abandoned apprentice works) he balances the two complementary tasks he sees as necessary for a Canadian novelist in his time—the adequate representation of the landscapes that surround and contain his characters, and the delineation of the other connected landscapes that exist within their minds. This can be observed at the beginning of each chapter in the way the visual setting is constructed with a truly Balzacian elaboration, so as to emphasize the almost symbolic relation that exists between the land, the city, and their human inhabitants. It is true that the overbearing presence of the environment seems excessive for an ordinary realistic novel; there is also too elaborate a pattern of coincidence to be credible in terms of ordinary verisimilitude. Both these characteristics fall into place when we realize that this is more than the mere story of an easily soluble mystery in the lives of a few human beings. The multiple significance of the imagery embraced in the landscape descriptions can be appreciated by taking a single paragraph from a point roughly a third of the way through the book, when Angus Murray stands waiting for a train in a moment of intense emotion.

The sky was bright with stars. Orion and Sirius stood over the forest, and the Bear, stretching a long arm to the northwest, rested above the Basin. The forest was hushed on the verge of winter storms, and the Basin, walled by darkness and illuminated by the stars, seemed filled to capacity with ships awaiting convoy. Their riding-lights flickered like a swarm of fireflies motionless in a void. Here Murray sensed an atomic quietness balanced at the core of constant change, of forces eternal and temporal about to radiate into areas where they would be drowned in a welter of predestined and controllable motion. The cold air was fresh with the smell of evergreens and of salt water, and in the far west there remained, like a tiny island burning with distant fire, a sliver of cloud still reflecting a glow from the sunken sun. (*BR*, 75)

Apart from the value of this description in setting the action concretely in the reader's mind, the passage conveys through its imagery a series of significant added nuances of meaning. The stars are repeated by the riding-lights of the ships, emphasizing the interconnection of human and cosmic levels of existence; darkness above and below, and the void in which the stars exist and the boats seem to float, enhance this impression of unity, which is made explicit in Murray's thought of "forces eternal and temporal," about to drown in "a welter of predestined and controllable motion"—an insight which of course foreshadows the titanic motion engendered by the explosion that will come within a few hours. The smells of evergreens and salt water project the peculiar physical characteristics of Nova Scotia, where one is always aware of the sea and the forest at the same time, but the cloud far to the west, "burning with distant fire," suggests the great land—one of the themes of the book—which stretches far beyond the borders of the Maritime provinces. But it has other meanings yet, for both west and fire connote hope and regeneration, while, in a final dimension, that burning island hung in the sky is prophetic of the fires that will later fall upon the city.

I have anticipated events in order to illustrate the way in which, throughout *Barometer Rising*, the imagery operates on a number of descriptive and symbolic levels, providing suggestive links between the different themes and lines of action which MacLennan is mingling for their mutual enhancement throughout the novel.

The young man who returns from exile, Neil MacRae, had been accused by his uncle Geoffrey Wain, also colonel of his battalion in France, of causing the failure of an attack. By chance the dugout in which MacRae had been imprisoned was bombed on the night before his court martial; he was given up for dead by his unit but found by a relieving battalion, taken back to England, and patched up without his real identity being found. Now he returns home, risking execution for cowardice, in the hope of finding the evidence that will clear his name. In Halifax is his cousin, Penelope Wain, with whom he was in love before he went away to the war; she, besides being—as he had hoped to become—a capable ship designer, is the daughter of Neil's enemy.

Wain and Penelope both learn of MacRae's presence in Halifax, and while the Colonel sets out to frustrate Neil's efforts and to get rid of him as quickly and un-obtrusively as possible, Penelope and Angus Murray, a wounded and hard-drinking M.O. who is in love with her, do their best to help MacRae vindicate himself. But the situation reaches its climax—a climax that is simul-taneously a catastrophe—not through the efforts of the two opposing parties, but as a result of the great explosion, which overshadows the whole latter half of the novel. MacRae and Murray both recover their self-respect and the respect of others through their superhuman feats in relieving the wounded, while Colonel Wain—found lying beside his naked secretary—is providentially among the dead. Meanwhile, Alec Mackenzie, a primitive giant of a Cape Breton fisherman who was Wain's batman in France and has been mortally injured in the explosion, gives Murray on his deathbed the evidence that will clear MacRae and enable him to marry Penelope and assume parenthood of their child.

The parallel between this story and that of the *Odyssey* is clearly shown not only in the name of the heroine, but also in MacRae's remark in the final chapter; "Wise Penelope! That's what Odysseus said to his wife when he got home. I don't think he ever told her he loved her. He probably knew the words would sound too small." But MacLennan not merely establishes in *Barometer Rising* a Homeric plot of the wanderer returning to a mysteriously changed homeland. He also uses for the first time a group of symbolic characters which will recur in various permutations in his later novels: the returning wanderer, the waiting woman, the fatherless child, the wise doctor— sometimes transformed into a wise old man—and the primitive, violent, but essentially good giant. If we wish to seek a Homeric parallel, the quintet of Odysseus, Penelope, Telemachus, Mentor and Eumaeus seems obvious, though MacLennan is too original a writer to follow the pattern slavishly, and we shall see the relationships of these five basic characters changing from novel to novel until, in *The Watch that Ends the Night*, the wanderer, wise old doctor and the primitive giant are finally united in that super-Odysseus, Jerome Martell.

The effective rendering of a universal myth adds to the effectiveness of a novel by extending a situation clasped in time into the shadows of the past, and linking it to symbolic patterns—in this case the journey as the way to wisdom and fulfilment—that are deeply lodged in the collective consciousness of man. In the case of *Barometer Rising*, the myth is used directly to reinforce the theme, which is the progression or "journey" of a country towards the point of self-consciousness in which it meets and recognizes its own destiny.

The idea of the First World War as a crucial point in this national journey is constantly reiterated. Canada is shown lying at a point of change, and the War is the agent that will bring that change about. Nova Scotia has a great past, but that age is gone, as Penelope realizes when she looks out from her office window into the ship-yard for which she works.

The shipyard was flooded with sunshine and the air reverberated with the savage striking of the riveting machines, punctuated occasionally with a ringing clang of heavy metals knocking together. The outlines of the ship they were building were gaunt and uncouth in this merciless light, and the workmen moving about her looked so small it was hard to realize they could be doing anything that mattered. Penny looked out of her window at this familiar scene and felt alien to it . . . (*BR*, 51)

Yet, despite herself, Penelope is one of the agents of

change, for she designs the extremely functional ship which the Admiralty accepts as a submarine chaser.

The fact that Penelope's talents are turned to the designing of weapons of destruction is an example of the dual character events and forces assume throughout the book. The war is destructive; it destroys men and ways of life. Yet it is also an agent of change, symbolized in the great troop carrier, the *Olympic,* which carries Canadians by thousands to the battlefields that will destroy or transform them, and each time returns to Halifax with a new camouflage, an altered guise which, of course, is echoed in that of Neil who returns with a changed nature and an assumed name.

Halifax, too, is changed by the war. Throughout the earlier part of the book the traditional links that connect Halifax with England rather than Canada are recognized, "it was her birthright to serve the British in time of war and to sleep neglected in time of peace" (*BR,* 33). Even those sceptical Nova Scotians like Murray who do not like the Englishmen they encounter and disapprove of Canadian policies being derived from British decisions, cannot shed the "intuitive belief that the best in England was the finest the world had yet seen, and that a world without England would be intolerable" (*BR,* 54).

But the war, for Halifax and by extension for Canada, is not merely a means to greater prosperity or a means of supporting the parent culture. It is also a force of revolution which the people "welcomed in the way a doctor welcomes the prospect of a dangerous operation" (*BR,* 143). Like all great negative events, it moves not according to the expectations of men: what is accidental in it is often more important than what is deliberate, and so the destruction that comes upon Halifax is of a totally unexpected kind. The invader steals into the harbour unobtrusively, in the shape of a shabby French freighter whose cargo of thousands of tons of munitions is exploded through collision with another ship and destroys by fire and blast, in the greatest wartime devastation before Hiroshima, the whole North End of the city. It is small wonder that to Neil and Murray "the catastrophe took on a cosmic aspect," and that Neil should afterwards think of the "abrupt and ruthless impingement of the unseen and the incalculable into his own life, the realization that what had happened today was not an adventure but a catastrophe."

An existentialist might have been content to use the Halifax explosion as a symbol of the absurdity which governs everything in that world where men can create significance only by shaping their own lives through a deliberate exercise of the power of choice in the infinity of random alternatives which chance offers. MacLennan, who believes in an intelligence controlling the universe, has something more than a striking phrase in mind when he speaks of the "cosmic aspect" of the explosion. He sees in the event at once the symbol and the instrument of inevitable change. It changes, literally, the life and shape of Halifax and the individual lives of thousands of people, whether they are killed or survive. It heralds the end of an old order and the beginning of a new consciousness. "Halifax," Penny thinks, "and with it the rigid, automatic life of her family's hierarchy, had been blown wide apart" (BR, 191). The explosion not only symbolizes the social revolution that brings an end to the rule of the Wains and to the old colonial order. It also represents creative forces. One of the most suggestive images in the book is that of the fires that descend from the sky.

> Over the North End of Halifax, immediately after the passage of the first pressure, the tormented air was laced with tongues of flame which roared and exploded out of the atmosphere, lashing downward like a myriad blow-torches as millions of cubic feet of gas took fire and exploded. The atmosphere went white-hot. It grew mottled, then fell to the streets like a crimson curtain. Almost before the last fragments began to fall, the wreckage of the wooden houses in the North End had begun to burn. (*BR*, 154)

The fire is a destructive element, but it is also a cleansing agent, since it clears the dirty, Dickensian slums of old Halifax, and there is a strange Pentecostal quality to that image of the tongues of fire lacing the tormented air, an image of regeneration. It appears from all the accounts of the Halifax explosion that burning gases did literally sweep down from the sky in this way, but MacLennan has used this extraordinary phenomenon for a number of symbolic purposes, just as he later uses the snow that fell over the town on the evening after the explosion, "the primal solitude of snow drifting like sand over the ruins," to suggest the process by which time heals the wounds of men and societies.

The Canadian social revolution which the explosion so catastrophically represents is present also in the relations between characters, and particularly between the three principal male characters. For the conflict between Geoffrey Wain and Neil MacRae into which Angus Murray is unwillingly drawn is not a mere personal quarrel. It personifies the struggle of two attitudes and two generations. Wain is a descendant of military colonists; he retains an essentially colonialist stance, since he despises the Nova Scotian world in which it has been his fortune to live. He remains tied to the British past and dominated by an ineffectual ambition to hold power and to become part of the military dictatorship which he sees as a logical end to the war. He represents outdated political ideas and an old hierarchy that must pass away if Canada is to live and grow as a nation.

Murray is—in a moral sense—the best man in the book; in creating him MacLennan has performed the unusual feat of delineating a thoroughly decent human being who is convincing and grows on one's appreciation with each reading of the novel. Murray, in whom MacLennan obviously buried a great deal of his father and a little of himself, has passed through suffering towards wisdom, in this anticipating Jerome Martell in *The Watch that Ends the Night*. He has abandoned ambition, and has come to the point where he can gracefully relinguish the promise of happiness, as he does when Neil returns to claim Penelope. "He thought now that a man could only know the meaning of peace when he no longer reached after the torment of hope" (*BR*, 143). He represents the Canadian caught between the two worlds of old colonial life and new national life, "intellectually gripped by the new and emotionally held by the old, too restless to remain at peace on the land and too contemptuous of bourgeois values to feel at ease in any city."

It is Neil, less wise but more impetuous and idealistic than Murray, who represents the new forces in Canada.

Since he was educated in Montreal, he has avoided the provincial outlook and has widened his patriotism from the local to the continental. "Here in Nova Scotia . . . he felt rooted and at home. Yet it had been in Montreal that all the good things had happened" (*BR*, 43-44). It is Neil who has the thoughts of Canada as a living whole. Waiting for a tram one day, he has a vision of the great sweep of Canada, with the railway line, that symbolic thread of unity, lying "with one end in the darkness of Nova Scotia and the other in the flush of a British Columbian noon."

Under the excitement of this idea his throat became constricted and he had a furious desire for expression: this anomalous land, this sprawling waste of timber and rock and water where the only living sounds were the footfalls of animals or the fantastic laughter of a loon, this empty tract of primordial silences and winds and erosions and shifting colours, this bead-like string of crude towns and cities tied by nothing but railway tracks, this nation undiscovered by the rest of the world and unknown to itself, these people neither American nor English, nor even sure what they wanted to be, this unborn mightiness, this question-mark, this future for himself, and for God knew how many millions of mankind! (*BR*, 79)

There are many satisfying things in *Barometer Rising*. The atmosphere—the very physical feeling—of Halifax four decades ago is admirably recreated, and the action moves with the right momentum towards the grand climax of the explosion. And this event is celebrated in reconstructive reporting which at the beginning of his career establishes the power of describing action in which MacLennan has always excelled. The description of what happened is accurate history without losing its impact on the imagination; indeed, *Barometer Rising,* among its other virtues, is one of Canada's few good historical novels. The later chapters telling of the rescue work are maintained at a level of sustained vigour, and the diminuendo from catastrophe to the saddened realization of human happiness when Neil and Penelope are finally and fully united gives the appropriate last touch to the novel's balance.

But these virtues, which make *Barometer Rising* a constantly interesting book, are balanced by defects which are due partly to deficiencies in technique and partly to Mac Lennan's view of life and the world. For example, the relationship between the lovers is the least convincing of all the links in the novel because of a curiously embarrassed clumsiness which makes MacLennan incapable of dealing with any aspect of sex except in high-mindedly sentimental terms. It would be hard to find anything more self-conscious, in an otherwise very naturally written book, than these paragraphs with which it draws to an end:

Suddenly Penny required his tenderness so greatly that it was as though all her life she had been starving for it. She wanted him to take her in his arms and hold her as he had done in that unbelievable night in Montreal when nothing had existed but sounds in the darkness and the sense that each of them had been born for that moment. All this she wanted, but the habit of restraint, the cold control she had trained herself to acquire, was still unbreakable.

Neil made no effort to move up the road. He stood watching her, then came close and his fingers touched her hair where it escaped over her temples. He gave a sudden smile, and all strain vanished from his face . . .

Tears welled up in her eyes and receded without overflowing and her fingers closed over his. He looked over her head to the patch of moonlight that broke and shivered in the centre of the Basin, and heard in the branches of the forest behind him the slight tremor of a rising wind. (*BR*, 219)

That does not strike one as felt emotion; it is too obviously cobbled in the mind of an embarrassed author out of the stock clichés of romanticist fiction—tears, moonlight, sudden smiles, fingers touching temples and wind rising in the forest. Here, at any rate, MacLennan learnt little from Homer.

More serious, because it seems to spring from a philosophic fatalism perennial in MacLennan's attitude, is the mechanical impetus that at times— and particularly during the explosion—takes the action wholly out of the characters' hands. MacLennan was a classical scholar before he became a novelist, and a Calvinist before he became a classicist, and the inexorable pattern of Greek tragedy still broods over his writing. Beyond a certain point, Penelope and Neil and Angus can no longer shape their fates. The apparent accident of the explosion takes on life and power to such an extent that Neil is really released from danger, not by proving his innocence, but because of the fortuitous justice of Geoffrey Wain, a man whose life was one extended *hubris,* being killed in a falling house.

The final flaw in *Barometer Rising* comes not from the concern of the major characters wth the destiny of Canada, but from the fact that this concern becomes articulate in the wrong way and often in the wrong situations. There are times when the theme assumes a crude and abstract form which tears like a jagged spur into the unity of both feeling and style. When, for instance, Neil and Penelope are leaving the devastated city, at a time when we might expect the warmly personal thoughts of two people united after many vicissitudes, we are all at once faced with this passage in Neil's thoughts.

Why was he glad to be back? It was so much more than a man could ever put into words. It was more than the idea that he was young enough to see a great country move into its destiny. . . . In returning home he knew that he was doing more than coming back to familiar surroundings. For better or worse he was entering the future, he was identifying himself with the still-hidden forces that were doomed to shape humanity as certainly as the tiny states of Europe had shaped the past. Canada was still hesitant . . . But if there were enough Canadians like himself, half-American and half-English, then the day was inevitable when the halves would join and his country would become the central arch which united the new order. (*BR*, 218)

Perhaps these are worthy sentiments of an awakening patriotism, but their expression at this particular point of fulfilment in Neil's emotional life makes him seem an inhumanly and improbably cold lover.

VII

THE ARCH OF UNITY

MacLennan's second novel, *Two Solitudes,* is dominated even more than *Barometer Rising* by the effort to give artistic shape to the author's vision of the arch of Canadian unity, and for this reason it stands with *The Precipice* and *Return of the Sphinx* as the three MacLennan novels least notable for their breadth of human understanding and their formal cohesion. Yet *Two Solitudes* enjoyed a public success, and to it rather than to *Barometer Rising* MacLennan owed his rapid elevation to the position of the most widely read and recognized Canadian novelist of his generation. As he has recollected, *Two Solitudes,* which was published in 1945, sold more copies in Canada than any Canadian novel since *Marie Chapdelaine.* Its success gave a first indication that in Canada writing might eventually become an economically viable profession, and reflected the intense preoccupation with national unity among the kind of English Canadians who read books and who were disturbed by the strain on Canadian unity caused by war-time conscription. As MacLennan remarked, "Literary merit had no connection with this sale; the book merely happened to put into words what hundreds of thousands of Canadians felt and knew" (SR, 266).

Two Solitudes is set almost entirely in Quebec, though the unity of place is not nearly so close as in *Barometer*

Rising, since in the latter part of the book there are interludes in Athens and on the coast of Maine. But the main action is contained between the poles of Montreal, the two-peopled centre of Canadian economic power, and Saint-Marc, a village by the St. Lawrence which when the novel begins in 1917 has already been touched by twentieth century progress. As in all of MacLennan's books, the sense of environment is particularly strong, and *Two Solitudes* actually opens with a geographical prelude to the action, describing the St. Lawrence valley, talking of its ancient villages and its great city ("If this sprawling half-continent has a heart, here it is . . ." [*TS*, 8]) and, in what we must recognize as a very Canadian way, sketching in the inhuman backdrop of the wilderness whose presence, like a figure in a recurrent drama, is undoubtedly the most constant factor in our literature.

The time of *Two Solitudes* is as extended as the terrain it covers. It begins in 1917, when conscription has become a divisive issue between English and French Canadians, and the first of the four unevenly sized parts into which the novel is divided takes place in that year and 1918; it occupies slightly more than half the book. The remaining three parts cover events scattered from 1919 to 1939; as the novel ends World War II is beginning. The events in Parts II, III and IV are consequent on those in Part I, and many of the characters persist throughout the book, but the central figure of Part I is the French Canadian politician, Athanase Tallard, and the central figure of the remainder of the book is his son, Paul. There is a sharp division, in mood as well as in structure, between Part I and the rest of the book.

Two Solitudes opens in Saint-Marc, which is dominated partly by the priest, Father Beaubien, and partly by the hereditary seigneur, Athanase Tallard. There has always been rivalry between priests and seigneurs in Saint-Marc, and Tallard is a politician—a federal M.P.—of anti-clerical inclinations. He is the most impressive character of the book because of his classically tragic predicament. He is not religious by nature and he does not have the ability to live according to the forms of a creed without concerning himself over its substance. In fact, he is a Voltairean rationalist. He is also a sensualist, and women mark the poles of his life, like the Sacred and Profane Loves of the renaissance painters. His first wife, Marie-Adèle, a girl of "delicacy and haunting innocence" whom he hopes to transform Pygmalion-like into a woman of the world, is one of the few members of her sex impervious to his charm. After giving birth to his first son, Marius, she retreats from her husband into pietism.

> She had gone to Mass every morning, and in the afternoon she could often be seen in church on her knees before the Virgin, with her hands clasped and her head thrown back in an ecstacy of admiration. (*TS*, 69)

While Marie-Adèle is still alive, Athanase encounters Kathleen Connors, an Irish hat-check girl of "earthy gentleness," who arouses and responds to his sensuality and eventually becomes his second wife. Here sensuality is revealed as Athanase's tragic flaw, for he sleeps with Kathleen on the night of his wife's death, his son Marius spies on him, and from this knowledge stems Athanase's later troubles.

71

As a politician, Athanase has been perpetually ineffectual, the M.P. who never quite made it into the cabinet, the man of good will whose fate is to be used by others. Like Geoffrey Wain, he has ambitions, but he lacks the power of mind to fulfil them. He believes quite sincerely that Quebec cannot stay in its agrarian slumber, and that if its people do not co-operate in the modernisation of their province, the English will do it against their will. He is in fact a kind of Quiet Revolutionist half a century ahead of his time, and there is a moment when he sees, like a vision in a mirror, the predicament of men of his kind.

> In every generation there arose French-Canadians who tried to change the eternal pattern of Quebec by political action, and nearly all of them had been broken, one by one. Indeed, they broke themselves, for while they fought for change with their minds, they opposed it with their emotions. If they went far enough, they were bound to find themselves ending with the British against their own people, and if nothing else broke them, that inevitably did. (*TS*, 71)

The latent conflict between Tallard and Father Beaubien, who represents traditional Quebec in its most obstinate form, only becomes acute when Tallard is the means, first of bringing the old Nova Scotian sea captain, John Yardley, to one of the farms in a village where no English have lived before, and then of co-operating with a group of English-Canadian financiers who are anxious to start a mill in Saint-Marc. The conflict is complicated by Tallard's relationship with his son Marius, who understandably resents his stepmother and at once hates and loves his father. In reaction against Athanase's policies, Marius becomes a fiery French-Canadian nationalist. He is arrested as a deserter, and this helps to arouse local hostility against his father. Finally, goaded by Father Beaubien's inflexible prejudices, Tallard renounces his Catholicism; he is boycotted by his neighbours, even his employees, and the English financiers who have induced him to set up the mill desert him and make their own arrangements with the bishop when they see that his unpopularity will harm their interests. Bankrupt and worn out with grief, he dies in Montreal; on his deathbed he returns to the Church—and his neighbours accept him when he is brought back, a failed Odysseus, to lie in their midst.

Behind the village, with its bitter conflicts of personality and principle, the English world of Montreal looms like a Kafkaesque fortress. There are two hierarchies, social and economic. At the head of the economic hierarchy stands the rarely seen and almost mythical Sir Rupert Irons, and somewhat lower down is Tallard's evil genius, Huntly McQueen, into whom MacLennan projects a great deal of what he saw in Mackenzie King; McQueen is astute in labour relations, has a passion for organization even more than for money, lives under the shadow of his mother's memory, and believes that Canada has "contrived to solve problems that would ruin other countries merely by ignoring them." One day, standing in a lift with Irons and three other financiers, McQueen has a sudden insight into the nature and power of Canada's élite which anticipates everything John Porter would say later in *The Vertical Mosaic*.

> The thought crossed his mind that if an accident had occurred between the first and second floors, half a million men would at that instant have lost their masters. It was an alarming thought. It was also ironic, for these individuals were so remote from the beings that governed, they operated with such cantilevered indirections, that they could all die at once without even ruffling the sleep of the remote employees on the distant end of the chain of cause and effect. The structure of interlocking directorates which governed the nation's finances, subject always to an exceptionally discreet parliament, seemed to McQueen so delicate that a puff of breath could make the whole edifice quiver. But no, McQueen smiled at his own thoughts, the structure was quite strong enough. The men who had risen together in the elevator this morning were so sound they seldom told even their wives what they thought or did or hoped to do. Indeed, Sir Rupert Irons was so careful he had no wife at all. They were Presbyterians to a man, they went to church regularly, and Irons was known to believe quite literally in predestination. (*TS*, 91)

Before *Two Solitudes* comes to an end we shall see that power of the economic élite not destroyed, but at least shaken by the rebellion of the young, and its ultimate vulnerability symbolized in the death of Sir Rupert Irons.

Higher on the slopes of Mount Royal than the financiers live such socially exclusive clans as the Methuens, the last generation of colonialists who, like the Wains of Halifax, despise their own country and live according to the standards of a British aristocracy that would snub them as outsiders. Incongruously linked with the Methuens is the earthy, garrulous Captain Yardley, whose daughter Jane, educated in an English-style finishing school, has married a Methuen. Jane has become even more snobbish than her husband's relatives, and eventually, a war widow, she inherits the great, gargoyle-ridden mansion. But Captain Yardley is wholly without social or national prejudices, and he settles into the village of Saint-Marc with such ease that the French like him against their wills, and continue to accept him even after Jane has horrified them by telling the police where Marius is hiding. He seems to belong to a world of pioneers, an almost Homeric world, dating from an age before the rivalry between peoples in Canada assumed its strident modern form. He provides the one enduring link between the world of Saint-Marc and that of Montreal, between Paul Tallard and his own grand-daughter Heather Methuen, who in the first part of the novel play together as children on his farm and in the later parts are brought together by him to become lovers and finally to marry.

In portraying the life of the rich English in Montreal, as in presenting that of landowner, priest and habitants in Saint-Marc, MacLennan is writing good social fiction, which makes us enter with understanding and even with a certain sympathy these little, alien and vanishing worlds. In the same way, he describes their settings, often with a lapidary exactness like that of good nature poetry, evoking poignantly the moods of the Laurentian countryside and the responses it arouses in his characters.

The first part of *Two Solitudes* is a close unity. It is dominated by the compelling tragedy of Athanase Tallard, and is bound together by the common anxieties of war and by the virtual identity of the larger problem of racial conflict with the actual lives and relationships of the characters. The problem seems to grow with the story rather than the story being fabricated to suit the problem, and the characters are up to this point well-knit and self-consistent. If *Two Solitudes* had ended with Tallard's death, it would have been artistically a moving and cohesive book. But didactically up to this point it merely presents the actual problem of relations between the English and the French; it does not have the logically neat completeness of an offered solution, and this task Mac-Lennan seeks, at the expense of his novel, to fulfil in its latter part.

After Tallard's death the action shifts almost entirely to Montreal, since all real links with Saint-Marc ended after his funeral there. Marius retreats into the shadows of French Montreal, where he ceases to change or develop and remains the type of the narrow Quebec nationalist. It is on his brother Paul that attention is now fixed—a Telemachus fated to complete his father's unfinished Odyssey, an actual wanderer over the seas and incidentally—like MacLennan—a dedicated reader of the original *Odyssey*. Paul's role is to span the races; half-French, half-Irish, he lives the rest of his childhood with his mother Kathleen, who knows no French. Ever since his father left the Church he has attended English schools; as he once says, he can speak English without a French accent and French without an English accent, and so personifies racial reconciliation. After the spoilt and sheltered child hood in Saint-Marc, he endures an impoverished youth. gets himself somehow through college (taking Greek in the process) and lives a depression existence of professional hockey games and odd jobs, sharing the anger of his time without the bitterness that marred so many in the Thirties.

Through Captain Yardley, whom he has been tutoring in Greek, Paul meets Heather Methuen once again; she is in revolt against the snobbery and materialism of her own environment, and it is in their growing relationship, representing the English and French, the Scottish and Irish ingredients in the Canadian national makeup, that the theme of the novel is taken up and personified. Indeed, it is in thinking of Heather, as he sits in Athens, that Paul first speaks in his mind the title phrase of the book. "He wondered if Heather had ever felt as he did now. Two solitudes in the infinite waste of loneliness under the sun" (*TS*, 260). When he gets home, he and Heather come together again, and, in spite of the machinations of her mother and the egregious Huntly McQueen, they are married and their marriage symbolizes a course which MacLennan hopes the peoples of Canada can follow, freeing themselves from old prejudices and hatreds, and coming together in the marriage of two solitudes. Finally, to show his hard-won sense of Canada as a united country, Paul defies his nationalist brother Marius, and voluntarily enlists to fight in the war that begins as *Two Solitudes* ends.

Neither Paul nor Heather is so well realized as the characters who dominate the earlier part of *Two Solitudes;* the very need to show them as flexible and capable of development gives them an indefiniteness of outline, compounded by the romantic vagueness with which the development of their relationship from friendship into love is handled. But perhaps the greatest weakness of the final chapters is that MacLennan—for the only time in his literary career—follows a modern fashion by making his hero a novelist who, like him, abandons as ineffectual a novel he has set in Europe, and turns to one which—like *Barometer Rising*—will show the developing consciousness within Canadians of their own country. This whole sub-theme of rising national consciousness as a subject for fiction fails from its own self-consciousness: MacLennan is speaking too personally. He is best when he gets away from the quasi-autobiographical vein, which induces too often a mood of clumsy coyness, and either uses documentary material in an objective way or transmutes personal experience through the use of his very considerable inventive powers.

MacLennan is so anxious to make his point about the reconciliation of the two Canadas that he is not content merely to show Paul with his dual ancestry as the obvious symbol of their union. At the end of *Two Solitudes* he actually steps out of the novelist's garment and assumes that of the social historian to deliver a final chapter of authorial reflection, not on the fate of his characters—a proper subject for a novelist to linger on—but on the destiny in wartime of the Canada they represent. He describes how, "quietly, without bands or parades, while advertisers warmed up to the slogans of 1914, the country moved into history as into matter-of-fact." And he goes on to finish the book in this way:

Then, even as the two race-legends woke again

remembering ancient enmities, there woke with them also the felt knowledge that together they had fought and survived one great war they had never made and that now they had entered another; that for nearly a hundred years the nation had been spread out on the top half of the continent over the powerhouse of the United States and still was there; that even if the legends were like oil and alcohol in the same bottle, the bottle had not been broken yet. And almost grudgingly, out of the instinct to do what was necessary, the country took the first irrevocable steps towards becoming herself, knowing against her will that she was not unique but like all the others, alone with history, with science, with the future. (*TS*, 319-20)

As an ending for a novel, all one can say of this passage is that it is a nullity, since any idea that is not from a sense of necessity revealed in the thought and speech and action of the character is redundant. Even Tolstoy when he broke this rule of the craft of fiction so grandly in *War and Peace*, doubling as novelist and historical philosopher, destroyed the unity of tone of his most ambitious book and greatly marred his final achievement. MacLennan in his turn reduces the ending of *Two Solitudes* to bathetic dullness by insisting on an author's last word.

The conclusion of *Two Solitudes* is in fact contrived to fit a nationalist message, and this divides it so sharply from the earlier chapters that, while the story of Athanase seems written by a novelist acutely sensitive to concrete human predicaments, the story of Paul reads as if it were written by a man in whom this very kind of sensitiveness had been wholly submerged under the abstractions of a destiny-ridden view of history. The division within the novel represents a dichotomy in MacLennan's literary view that he has never completely overcome.

VIII

MARIPOSA AND MEGALOPOLIS

Of all Hugh MacLennan's novels, the least satisfying has been *The Precipice,* and the reason for its weakness is almost certainly the fact that in writing it he abandoned the resolution he had taken on beginning *Barometer Rising,* and decided to set a large portion of the book in the United States. For a writer whose literary antennae are so closely attuned to his native society and its special moral nuances, it was a risky decision to take, and the result is a novel which, while not entirely without the merits that one expects in any work of a sensitive observer and a good craftsman, must be regarded as a failure in the sense that it is neither convincing nor self-consistent. When he was writing *The Precipice* MacLennan thought his American experiences had made it "inevitable." Yet inevitability is the last quality that springs to one's mind on reading *The Precipice,* particularly in comparison with *Barometer Rising* and *Each Man's Son,* both of which seem to respond to commanding voices within the author's deeper consciousness. None of his books seems more contrived or more mechanical than *The Precipice.*

In *The Precipice* the life of Grenville, an innocent and narrow-minded lakeside town of Ontario, is shown in contrast to the "precipice" of New York, which attracts so many unwitting Canadians to moral destruction, and destroys so many more of its own. It is the only novel in which MacLennan's principal character is a woman, and —while it is a brave effort of its kind—his inability to portray the feminine nature with any profundity (an inability that may well be linked with the Calvinist inhibitions he touches on in this book and later analyzes so well in *Each Man's Son*) is undoubtedly one of the principal reasons for its failure.

To put the matter of the novel in bold and sketchy lines, the heroine, Lucy Cameron, is a mousy Jane Austenish young woman (without the acerbly ironic Austen view of her fellow beings), caught in the narrow interests of her community and apparently destined to a perpetual spinsterhood, tempered by an interest in the kind of writing (e.g., Aldous Huxley) considered risqué in such environments in the 1930's, and by a love of gardens which gives her the mildly mythical flavour of a suburban Flora. This destiny is averted when she meets a visiting American businessman, Stephen Lassiter. Under his influence she blossoms phenomenally—plainness changing under Pygmalion-like stimulation into breathtaking beauty is a predictable attribute to the MacLennan heroine. Eventually she runs away from her disapproving elder sister, the puritanical Jane, and marries Stephen in an American village. They live in New York where Stephen becomes involved in that lowest circle of the American inferno, the advertising world, until—despite Lucy's efforts to counter the baleful influence of megalopolitan life—the marriage almost shatters. Lucy retires to Grenville with her children. Stephen sets off on his miserable Odyssey, succumbing to over-educated sirens, running on the rocks of business failure, until his nerve breaks and he is reunited with Lucy in a happy ending of excruciating banality, meeting again under the shadow of Hiroshima's destruction, in "a strange hotel in a strange city, bare of reminders of the past" (*P*, 365).

Such, if one were called upon to summarize *The Precipice* briefly, is the kind of rapid analysis it would be impossible to avoid. Yet it is not wholly a bad book. It starts with deceptive spirit. The early chapters—beginning in 1938 when "Canada breathed out the last minutes of her long Victorian sleep" (*P*, 3)—describe the small-town life of the three sisters in a way that is alive, self-consistent and perceptive. In the library run by the Daughters of the Empire and at the boat-club dance, in the drug-store and in the churches and in the home of the Cameron girls, life is authentically portrayed, a life which in some corners of some Ontario towns lingers even twenty years after MacLennan wrote and which leaves one wondering, as Lucy herself once wonders, where "all the violence" that characterized the past of Ontario has vanished.

In fact it has not entirely vanished. It has been submerged under the "glaze of respectability," under the frost of puritanism. But, though Grenville "glorifies the commonplace at the expense of the exceptional" (*P*, 165), so that, as Lucy observes, "personal freedom could rest only on a bad reputation" (*P*, 17), those of sturdily bad reputations do persist there, one of the most flourishing being Lucy's uncle, Matt McCunn, renegade from Presbyterian ministry into anti-puritan bohemianism. "So long as there were people anywhere who rejected the idea of success, he was with them" (*P*, 236). Matt, with his earthy talk and his search for a natural uninhibited life, proffers the same kind of wisdom as Angus Murray and Captain Yardley, and he is one of the two men in Grenville who recognizes in Lucy the beauty that is hidden under her demure dress, and the passion that is sublimated in her devotion to flowers.

The other is Bruce Fraser, the quintessential Canadian of the Thirties, typical of the "wistful, waiting" aspect of Grenville, of Canada in transition. The leading characters in all MacLennan's novels, up to and including *Each Man's Son,* are children of villages or small towns, but they—and often their towns as well—are in the process of becoming urbanized. Grenville begins that process when the American financiers move in to take over its one factory (one of MacLennan's many anticipations in fiction of issues that later became potent in fact). Bruce himself is in the process of being urbanized, living between the sleepy summer world of a soberer Mariposa and the frenzied, committed city world of the Thirties. Like his country, he gropes through depression and war towards a realization of his own true nature. But he allows Lucy to slip away from him when he might have her, and when he is mature enough to demand her she is not free to be taken. Perhaps in that contrary destiny there is a deep comment on the nature of Canadians.

The purpose Bruce performs in *The Precipice* is essentially that of chorus. He observes and defines Lucy's possibilities, but in their liberation his only function is to assist her to escape to marry the American Stephen Lassiter. When Lucy lives with Lassiter in New York it is Bruce who sees her flowering in that foetid jungle. And when she leaves Stephen it is Bruce again who observes her state of mind, who helps her unwillingly to clarify the issues that perplex her, and who watches her receding again out of his grasp as she rejoins her husband.

The paradox of Lucy's escape is that she flees to what she has sought to lose. When Stephen first comes into her view, an over-sized American playing tennis with his diminutive and demoniac friend, Carl Bratian, Grenville seems to her "a smaller place than it had seemed half an hour ago" (P, 21), and Stephen becomes not only a man to love but also a means to free herself from the life that has frozen her "into the mould of a perpetual childhood" (P, 19). Like many of MacLennan's women, the immediate force from which Lucy seeks escape is her elder sister, Jane, custodian of the harsh puritanical ideals on which the departed John Knox Cameron had modelled his household and set the course of his daughters' lives. Jane is not inwardly dead; far from it. But her passion is sublimated in the music she teaches and only occasionally expressed with astonishing sultriness when she plays Beethoven in moments of high tension. At other times she seems the model of controlled puritanism.

> She was the only one of them who followed, in thought and in life, all the principles of the religion and morality which the entire Protestant part of the country professed to honour. The great crimes had no reality for her whatever. She had never in her life seen an act of deliberate wickedness. It was natural to her to believe that sex was the dirtiest thing in the world, and near to the root of all evil. (P, 122)

The great balancing act which MacLennan attempts in *The Precipice* is to demonstrate that Jane and Stephen, who detest each other and seem poles apart, are really siblings under the skin, the end products of paths branching off from the same "journey which the puritans began more than three hundred years ago when they lost hope in themselves and decided to bet their lives on the things they could do rather than the men they were" (P, viii). Jane values more than anything else correct behaviour; so, in his way, does Stephen, but for him the correct behaviour is that which proves his manliness and leads to the material rewards of success. Yet it is a barren journey on to which his hard, materialistic and moralistic ancestors have put him, as barren as that which condemns Jane to her indurated spinsterhood, and the essential futility of this aspect of American life is symbolised when Stephen and Lucy are travelling across the United States and come, far out in Kansas, to a dust-ruined ghost town, Lassiter City, founded by Stephen's grandfather in the mid-nineteenth century.

Stephen had hunted for the graveyard, found it near a bleached and cracked wooden church, and Lucy had jumped back as a copper-coloured bull snake crawled away from a headstone. "Thomas Lassiter— Founder of this Town. Born 1827—Died 1899." . . . . The place had moved Lucy far more than it moved Stephen. She learned then a little of what it meant to be an American with a press of lonely, hopeful men behind you, still carrying within yourself something of the belief which had brought Thomas Lassiter here from Missouri, and his father to Missouri from Ohio, and behind him the long line of lean men threading west out of New England, no poetry

86

in them, no music, but the necessity of believing that westward things were better, over every mountain a valley richer than the last, carrying wherever they went the qualities that made them unlike any other people who had ever lived, the great refusal to be satisfied, to rest and sit down, the unwillingness to be content which was as hard as a rock in the soul. First the Lord had hounded them, and when the Lord grew remote, they had hounded themselves. (P, 277-8)

And Stephen, under the skin of his apparent hedonism as ridden a puritan as any, hounds himself like his ancestors. Tempted by the Mephistopheles of the novel, Carl Bratian, he strives for success and money in the meretricious world of advertising, embittered that he could not be an engineer and mortified that, despite his fine physique, the army doctors find defects enough to keep him out of action. New York becomes the hostile wilderness in which he seeks his false grails, and in its diabolical atmosphere Lucy, blossom though she may into a suave and sophisticated woman, cannot help him. He must find himself.

This American centre of the novel tells a tale of metropolitan corruption that has been told often before, and MacLennan brings no fresh light to illuminate it. It is a tourist's eye view of the city that he presents, and among the brassy glitter of familiar clichés about its life, the sense of an original world, which existed when he wrote of Grenville, disappears. The novel slumps into a stock romance in which Lucy, now a smug and irritating paragon, loyally supports Stephen, changed into a comic caricature of the ulcered adman, and finally, after his many betrayals, and after leaving him to return to Grenville, nobly forgives all and consoles him in his downfall.

It is this collapse in authenticity when we go from Grenville to New York and Princeton that mars the self-consistency of *The Precipice*. It is not that MacLennan is without good insights. When Lucy goes away from Princeton, it is because she too realizes how false her life has become under that veneer of self-sufficiency which so deceives Bruce Fraser in New York. And when she returns to Stephen it is because at last he has embarked on the discovery of his true self. Unlike his father, unlike so many other Americans, he stops short of the precipice that is the end of the journey by the dusty way of Lassiter City. But these good things are lost in a morass of sentimentality, melodrama and moralizing, so that often the American chapters of *The Precipice* remind one of a Victorian cautionary novel. As tract-writing no doubt this is admirable; as fiction it is dull and, worse, unconvincing.

The fault lies in the attempt to enforce a lesson, or, rather, two lessons, that of the dangers of the puritan state of mind, and that of the relationship between Canada and the United States, which MacLennan likens to that between a woman and a man. There is a wry accuracy in the ascription of femininity to the Canadian character, but, again, the failure to bring this view into convincing focus lies in the essential unacceptability of Lucy as a credible character in her own right. One has only to compare her with Brian Moore's Mary Dunne—another Canadian girl lost in megalopolis—to realize how incredible, even in fictional terms, she really is.

One observes in *The Precipice*, as in *Two Solitudes*,

how far the effort to work out moral and social problems in logical terms tends to weaken the mythical structure that MacLennan brings forward from *Barometer Rising*. In each of these intermediate novels we encounter again the Odyssean pattern of journey and return, and also, at least in part, the Homeric group of characters. But both plot and characters lose strength when MacLennan seeks to state explicitly what should be suggested figuratively. And so the returns of Paul Tallard and Stephen Lassiter are less moving and less convincing than the return of Neil MacRae because they contain no element of mystery; nothing can grow from them in the imagination because we know far too clearly what the author wishes them to mean.

IX

HOMER AND CALVIN

In contrast to the novels that preceded it, *Each Man's Son* is a tensely constructed, unified book in which the balance of theme and mythical structure is re-established. Central to the novel is the tragedy of the failing boxer, Archie MacNeil, and in the portrayal of Archie's world of prize fights, shabby gymnasia and rascally promoters, MacLennan writes once again with a descriptive power equal to that developed in the account of the explosion in *Barometer Rising*; he has often written well on sports in his essays, and there are passages in the training and boxing sequences of *Each Man's Son* which not only evoke violent action as visibly as anything Hemingway wrote on boxers and boxing, but also show a remarkable understanding of the mind of a gentle man who lives by fighting.

Yet Archie's fate and its lurid ending, the fate of a basically good primitive in an environment of cynical exploitation, does not represent the only or, indeed, the principal theme of the novel, though to a great extent *Each Man's Son* is a threnody on the old Highland culture, on the "blasphemy," as one character calls it, of "fighting clans going into the blackness of the earth to dig coal." Even stronger is the theme of Calvinist guilt, which afflicts Archie and all the other people of the little Cape Breton mining town of Broughton but which appears most dramatically in the conflicts that plague Daniel Ainslie, the brilliant surgeon whom conscience prevents from ever fulfilling his promise as a doctor and a man.

In MacLennan's essays, the curse of a puritanical religion which induces a haunting sense of guilt is shown as the principal internal enemy of our western civilization. As a novelist, of course, MacLennan makes such generalizations only by implication, yet there is no doubt that Ainslie and the other Highlanders are in this sense meant to appear as representatives of Protestant culture as a whole, albeit in their case the sickness takes a somewhat extreme form. As MacLennan explains in the Author's Note which he, a born essayist, could not resist attaching to give his ideas literal and explicit expression:

> To Cape Breton the Highlanders brought more than the Quixotic gallantry and softness of manner belonging to a Homeric people. They also brought with them an ancient curse, intensified by John Calvin and branded upon their souls by John Knox and his successors—the belief that man has inherited from Adam a nature so sinful that there is no hope for him and that, furthermore, he lives and dies under the wrath of an arbitrary God who will forgive only a handful of his elect on the Day of Judgment. (*EM*, viii).

Archie who wanders and tragically returns, and Daniel Ainslie whose inner restlessness sends him journeying as the novel ends, are both (though intellectually poles apart) subject to the fate of that "fighting race with poetry in their hearts and a curse upon their souls. Each Man's Son was driven by the daemon of his own hope and imagination—by his energy or by his fear—to unknown destinations" (*EM*, ix). None is exempt; even Ainslie, free thinker and classicist, his mind filled with the liberating light of ancient Greece, is still, unknown to himself, haunted "every day of his life . . . by a sense of sin, a legacy of the ancient curse" (*EM*, ix).

In period, *Each Man's Son* is the earliest of Mac-Lennan's books, its action contained in the year 1913. Its setting is the setting of MacLennan's own Cape Breton childhood, and one can reasonably assume that fictional Broughton contains a great deal of its creator's memories of factual Glace Bay. Daniel Ainslie, a doctor in the mines and a dedicated student of Homer, certainly carries some of the attributes of MacLennan's father. And the setting is imbued with that Homeric light which Mac-Lennan himself remembers as characterizing the rural Nova Scotia of his youth, a light that not only gives a classical quality to the landscapes, with their streams and rivers and seas strangely magical in a child's perception, but also portrays the miners as a people who still retain those traits of the primitive Celt which made the Highlands before Culloden one of the last refuges of a Homeric way of life. There is the intuitive sense by which one Celt understands what occurs in the mind of another (and the sophisticated Ainslie has this as much as his simpler neighbours). There is the sense of a fate hanging over them which makes ill-luck expected and good fortune suspect. There is a state of mind in which "physical courage had become the only virtue." And in this setting many of the characters become inevitably either caricatures or humble projections into a degenerated modern world of Homer's heroes and heroines. Red Willie Mac-Isaac is a grotesque descendant of bully Achilles, in Magistrate MacKeegan Agamemnon descends to the level of burlesque, and Mrs. MacCuish talks in the deranged voice of prophecy like a decayed Cassandra. It is a setting where violence, superstition, and a consciousness of guilt and doom belong so naturally that MacLennan is able to present them without melodrama and with a naturalness that is not unconnected with the fact that so much is obviously derived from the stirring of childhood memories.

The structure within which MacLennan develops his two themes differs considerably from that used in *Two Solitudes* and *The Precipice*. In each of those intermediate novels he allowed the statement of a problem to be followed in chronological sequence by its solution, and the result was a linear pattern whose lack of inner tension undoubtedly contributed to the anti-climax into which both books inevitably fall. In *Each Man's Son* MacLennan returns emphatically—even if unconsciously —to the counter-pointed pattern of the *Odyssey*. Life in the Cape Breton village, where Archie's wife Mollie and her son Alan awaits his return, alternates with Archie's own wandering adventures, just as life on Ithaca alternates with the distant wanderings of Odysseus. There are touches which—if we accept MacLennan's statements that he did not consciously follow the model of the *Odyssey*— are astonishing examples of the working of the literary unconscious. Molly, like Penelope, is working on a tapestry—or at least, a carpet on a loom. Alan, like Telemachus, is highly conscious of a father who "has gone out into the world" (*EM*, 6), and of being "son of the bravest man in Cape Breton" (*EM*, 10), just as Telemachus is conscious of being son of the bravest man on Ithaca. Archie has been away four years, he has sent no money for a year, he has not written for eight months, yet it is only now that Mollie, like Penelope at the beginning of the Greek epic, begins to feel that he may not return and that she may be forced into choosing another mate.

The temptations to which Mollie is subject are, indeed, more complex than those which her numerous suitors impose upon Penelope. It is true that literally she has only one instead of many suitors, and that is the "Frenchman from France," Louis Camire. Camire is important not only as a catalytic factor, who precipitates the catastrophe that occupies such a classic position within the novel; he is also thematically important as the only leading character who comes from a non-Protestant and essentially sophisticated culture. Camire represents the European classical culture which has made its terms with pagan values, and his desires are natural and direct. Yet he is an unpleasant little man, for he has desire but no love, and is unable to conceive a world not governed by the key phrase of his philosophy: "Nobody does something for anybody without they want something back." He is a perverted product of the doctrines of class struggle that in the early twentieth century were agitating the masses of Europe, and thus he contrasts with the Cape Breton Highlanders, who think of themselves not in class terms, but rather as a homogeneous society in which degree exists, but no antagonism bred of it. The miners, as fellow Celts, accept Daniel Ainslie, even though there is a divergence in prosperity and in ways of life between them.

Between Camire, who hopes to become Mollie's lover, and Daniel Ainslie, there is not only a profound gulf in terms of origin and attitude but there is also a profound hostility, partly because Camire does not share the respect which the miners accord the doctor, and partly because Ainslie lays his own claim to Mollie.

Ainslie is a man of complex mental agony. He is a splendid doctor, and in the hospital he is always confident, a man in "his own world where his skill had made him a master" (*EM*, 43). It is the only place where he does not feel sadness and frustration, where he does not seem to others masterful and inconsiderate (a man with "a diamond in place of a heart"—(*EM*, 26), where he does not feel the fear of the curse that "led directly to a fear of love itself" (*EM*, 219). The curse takes material form in Ainslie's personal life.

> He was past forty, he had no children, he was in a treadmill, which he could neither slow down nor escape by jumping off, and Margaret's unhappiness made him feel increasingly guilty day by day. (*EM*, 54)

Margaret, his wife, comes of an earlier tradition than that of the Highlands. She belongs to an old Yankee Loyalist family, settled in Nova Scotia, once prosperous owners of sailing boats, and still given to a carefree life in which, unlike her husband, they "were always ready to take the easy way out of a situation" (*EM*, 39). Where Daniel is constantly analysing his situation, his actions and his motives, Margaret is inclined to follow her mother's teaching that "sensible people get rid of their troubles by laughing at them" (*EM*, 170).

She is always ready to soothe Daniel's frustrations by the simple therapy of love-making. But inevitably she is drawn into the circle of his agony. In the beginning of their marriage, Daniel had felt it premature to have children. Then Margaret suffered an illness which forced him to perform an operation that made her incapable of child-bearing. Always, in her mind, there is the haunting, unjust suspicion that the operation was done unnecessarily, and her unhappiness derives from the consciousness of Daniel's longing to have a son which as Dr. Dugald MacKenzie, his old friend and the Nestor of the novel, tells him is really a religious desire. "You aren't looking for a son, Dan. You're looking for a God."

Daniel's desire for a son, and Margaret's involvement in it, lead towards the catastrophe of the novel. For it is upon Alan, Archie's child, that his hovering and frustrated love at last alights. The idea first occurs to him on a day when he goes to Louisburg to perform an operation. Mollie and Alan are on the train and he insists on showing them the ruins of the fortress, that monument to past dreams of power over which the grass has grown and re-established, as in so many places of Cape Breton, the reign of ultimately untameable nature. As such, it appears in *Each Man's Son* as a symbol of regeneration (the brilliant operation Ainslie has just performed has given life to a man expected to die), and it is here that he comes to a realization that will be decisive in the lives of many people.

> . . . The realization began to grow in him that if he had a son like Alan MacNeil he would be content

to live and work anywhere, even in Broughton. But as soon as the idea was fully formed and he began to inspect its implications, he discarded it. Again something seemed to turn over within his chest and he was afraid of the feeling. Habit came to his rescue and he forced himself to think as a doctor. He told himself that it was a crime for a boy such as Alan to be raised with no future but the mines. Any man with a simple sense of humanity would do what he could to prevent such a boy from being sent into the pits. It was only his plain duty to do what he could. (*EM*, 133-4)

For a time Daniel masks his feelings from himself, and is content with advising Mollie not to join Archie, who has written to her from Trenton in New Jersey, where he will fight his last fight and meet his decisive defeat as a boxer. She is troubled by the advice, but acts upon it, and this contributes to Archie's downfall, and to the eventual tragedy.

It is when Alan is dangerously ill shortly afterwards that Daniel's feelings come surging to the surface. In saving the boy's life, it seems as though he has made him his own, and that here is the answer to all his longings. As soon as he has performed the operation he goes out to the seashore and the pounding surf to do battle with his feelings.

How long before he was able to say it quietly to himself he could not tell. But after he had said it again and again, it was his and he was no longer afraid of it. His life was a barrenness because he had no son. And now a son had been found.

There it was. All of it. It made no difference that Alan was the child of two people as dissimilar from himself and Margaret as were Archie and Mollie MacNeil. A man's son is the boy he himself might have been, the future he can no longer attain. For him, Alan was that boy. (*EM*, 183)

During Alan's convalescence Daniel subtly tries to exert a domination over the boy, and after he leaves the hospital arranges for him to go every day to his house for meals and tuition. Both Mollie and Margaret are disturbed, the one fearing the loss of her son's affection and the other the loss of her husband's, and Margaret unthinkingly advises Mollie not to ignore Camire's proposal to take her and Alan away to France. Mollie refuses to let Alan go to the Ainslie house any more, and this is a partial triumph for Camire, who has been feeding her resentment of Daniel. In the end she listens to the Frenchman's other urgings.

But the night Mollie gives herself to Camire is also the night on which the two paths of *Each Man's Son* run together, and the wanderer returns, a man wrecked by too many fights and going blind, but not too blind to see what is going on when he opens the cottage door. So, in miniature, the slaughter in the great hall of Ithaca is repeated. Archie kills Camire, mortally wounds Mollie who has tried to stop him, and falls in a stroke from which he quickly dies. Alan, the terrified witness of it all, is left completely alone, and, now that all the intervening characters have so providentially been swept away in a catastrophe of Jacobean proportions, Ainslie can at last combine the roles of doctor and father and claim the boy as his own.

The tragedy is almost grotesquely inevitable, and it gives a certain disproportion to *Each Man's Son*, since it is the bloody scene in the cottage—following on the mayhem of Archie's last fight—that remains most vividly in one's mind. Archie's somewhat melodramatic history tends to take unintended precedence over Daniel's inner agony which is the main subject of the novel, just as his guilt—representing that of the Protestant world in general—is its main theme, and his progress in the last pages through fear and horror to real love is its conclusion.

As in his earlier works, MacLennan in *Each Man's Son* cannot avoid seeing life running in the lines of Greek tragedy, and the mechanics of a classical destiny do seem to grind their pattern too heavily and harshly on the human weakness of his characters. Yet this incorporation of destiny, with its corresponding weakening of the sense of human freedom, is not entirely inappropriate in a novel so permeated with the ambient darkness of Calvinist guilt. For the people MacLennan creates, as for the actual Cape Bretoners among whom he grew up, destiny is an inner reality, and so for once the novelist's own fatalism is in tune with his subject. MacLennan does suggest with powerful effectiveness the fear that always seems to overtop hope in the hearts of these displaced clansmen, and he portrays equally effectively the relationships of degrees and persons in a little society bound together by a common faith in its own damnation. It is likely that the immediacy one feels in *Each Man's Son* (rivalled only in *Barometer Rising*) and the tension that unites structure and theme and myth, and makes the characters convincingly human even when they are most the slaves of circumstance, stem from their closeness to his own experience.

X

ODYSSEUS EVER RETURNING

The Watch that Ends the Night is MacLennan's largest
and most ambitious novel. It has faults and virtues propor-
tionate to its position as the peak of his achievements up
to the present; it is at once his most successful social novel
and his most brilliant failure in the proper function of a
novelist, which is to present human relationships that in
their own terms are convincing. Beyond both these dimen-
sions, it moves on to a philosophic plane in which the
wider political and metaphysical problems that have af-
flicted the generations from the Thirties onwards are
worked out with a painstaking intensiveness rare among
Canadian writers. It is a novel large in texture and intention, and of the classic nineteenth century tradition, for
it is the one novel in which MacLennan, like Dickens
and Balzac—and also like H. G. Wells in his non-scientific
vein—successfully projects the comedy and the complexity
as well as the pathos and the tragedy that are inherent in
any social landscape.

Within the first few pages the pattern of echoes that
rings throughout MacLennan's novels is set going, and we
are reminded of *Barometer Rising,* for here again a
revenant comes back from the battles of life and the
shadows of death to the haunt of his youth and the
woman he has left waiting. But, once beyond this common starting point, MacLennan's first and his fifth novel

diverge on separate errands. In *Barometer Rising* the action really revolves around the efforts of Neil MacRae to claim his rightful place among the living. But Jerome Martell in *The Watch that Ends the Night* comes home from the Nazi torture chambers—by way of a long pilgrimage through Russia and China—only, like the original Odysseus, to renew his wanderings. His return, in fact, is important most of all for its effect on his former wife Catherine and on George Stewart, the lover from childhood whom she married after hearing the false news of Martell's death. For years Catherine and George have lived in the quiet campus security of a present that seems sealed from the more destructive acids of memory. And then George rings up a number the college porter has given him and—as he hears Jerome's forgotten voice—finds himself in the echoing tunnel of memory that leads towards a past he had thought done with for ever.

By this means *The Watch that Ends the Night* becomes a novel constructed in receding vistas of time, and in handling the leaps of memory MacLennan's craftsmanship is unobtrusively sure. We retreat with George in his role of narrator, first into the childhood in which, by regarding sickly Catherine with her rheumatic heart as a girl rather than an invalid, he gives her the confidence of her own feminity that will make her into a good wife for Jerome and later for himself. Time surges forward to the Thirties, the Depression and Spain and the Leftist Dream, and Jerome appears with them, an idealistic surgeon, deft with a scalpel and crushing with an argument or a fist, sweeping Catherine into marriage on the first evening he takes any notice of her, a figure larger than life who now bursts dramatically into George's memory in the middle of that fateful telephone conversation as once he exploded into the quietness of Montreal English society.

Jerome, though not technically the hero of *The Watch that Ends the Night*, is a figure in the heroic mould, the wanderer and the giant and the medicine man all in one, an energumen in the Thirties, a man of sorrows and saintly wisdom in the Fifties, who seems for most of the novel too far above common clay to be either true or tolerable unless we accept him as myth incarnate (and there is a good deal of reason to do so). Yet there are points in which even Jerome becomes authentically human, and most of all when another tunnel of time opens up, and takes us back in the middle of the novel, to the New Brunswick woods in the first years of the century, and the childhood of a boy born of an illiterate European immigrant woman and brought up in the primitive logging camps where his mother works as cook; he does not know his father or any name for himself but Jerome. His mother is murdered almost before his eyes by one of her lovers; evading the killer, Jerome escapes down river and is adopted by a simple-minded pastor and his wife who find him starving in the Moncton railway station. His later childhood, like MacLennan's, is passed in Halifax.

This part of *The Watch that Ends the Night* is written as admirably as MacLennan has ever written of primitive action. The woods of New Brunswick take shape in one's mind as a distinct physical presence, different from any other woods one has ever read of or walked in, and the night scene in the sleeping camp when the boy escapes from the murderer is powerfully thrilling.

At the end of *The Watch that Ends the Night* Jerome —now a man whose very face has gone transparent with experience and whose eyes seem "to have seen everything, known everything, suffered everything" (*WE*, 361)— dispenses his wisdom and departs for the West. The shock of his return has shortened Catherine's life so that she is now an obviously dying woman—"living her death" as Jerome expresses it—but the returning wanderer has enabled her and George to find themselves, to face their pasts, and to wait tranquilly in a world of gathering shadows for death. In fact, in a sense Jerome has passed them through death, and so the three main characters become united at that key point of the Odysseus myth, the descent into the underworld that precedes rebirth into the sunlight.

There is a flavour of pietistic smugness about this ending which is hard to accept, though—as I hope to show— the philosophic implications are not necessarily so. There is also, throughout *The Watch that Ends the Night*, a suave mawkishness in talking about sex which amounts almost to diplomatic evasion; in this respect it is a regression on *Each Man's Son*, and suggests how far MacLennan still suffers from his Calvinist background. But granting such shortcomings, *The Watch that Ends the Night* is still a novel that impresses one for its craftsmanship, its ambitious grasp of Canadian social situations, and its philosophic largeness.

The quality of the craftsmanship appears in the admirable construction of the novel, and in MacLennan's thoroughly workmanlike (though not especially original) manipulation of time recessions and shifts of scene, so that the interconnections of phases and places within a half-century of Canadian life are admirably delineated (though MacLennan's Canadian view is limited here, as in his other novels, by the total exclusion of anything that happens west of Ontario). It is evident also in the passages of capable description that punctuate the book, not only when action is involved but equally in the presentation of scenes that set moods—scenes in the wilderness and the city alike:

> I sat in silence staring at the landscape which stared back: form and colour and light and shade, useless to farmers, some of the oldest rock in the world cropping out of it, dark green and light green, ancient, mindless, from everlasting to everlasting without any purpose anyone could possibly understand, but there. (*WE*, 265)

> Never before was Montreal as it was in the Thirties and it will never be like that again. The unemployed used to flow in two rivers along St. Catherine Street, and I used to see eddies of them stopping in front of shop windows to stare at the goods they could not buy. There was a restaurant that used to roast chickens in its window over electrically operated spits, and there were always slavering men outside staring at the crinkling skin of the chickens and the sputtering fat. I remember how silent the unemployed were when they emerged after a snowfall to clean the streets, often without mittens on their hands, and how pitiful their cheap worn shoes looked as the snow wet them, and turned the unpolished leather grey. (*WE*, 119)

The least sure craftsmanship appears in the dialogue. In casual, peripheral or comic situations the speech of his characters is often fitting and natural, but in emotional situations, which abound in *The Watch that Ends the Night*, it tends to become hollow and pretentious, with rhetoric taking the place of feeling.

In social terms *The Watch that Ends the Night* is a great deal more than a celebration of Montreal, though that it undoubtedly is, presenting with impressionist vividness the city of George's youth (André Siegfried's "English garrison encysted in an overgrown French village"), and then the Montreal of drab distress and political tension in the Thirties, and finally the shining metropolis of the Fifties, "the subtlest and most intricate city in North America" (*WE*, 255). It is true that one has only to compare *The Watch that Ends the Night* with Mordecai Richler's *Son of a Smaller Hero* or *The Apprenticeship of Duddy Kravitz* to realise that MacLennan has not acquired the intensive knowledge of special ways of living that comes only from childhood experience, but he has a feeling for the relationships between groups on a broader scale, and his evocation of the changing character of English Montreal has a real inner consistency. But it is not only the grasp of personal and power relationships within a portion of the city circumscribed by class and language that is impressive; MacLennan also presents with memorable vividness a variety of Canadian social set pieces, from the CBC and the Ministry of External Affairs to a primitive New Brunswick logging camp, a Halifax manse, and a set of party-lining academics. Perhaps the best of these vignettes is that of Waterloo College, a school run by eccentric Englishmen which represents the novel's high point of social comedy and MacLennan's peak of ironic deprecatory humour.

Like great winds the collective passions of the decades sweep through these little worlds, and it is in the Thirties that the passions are strongest. "The Thirties lie behind us like the memory of guilt and shame," says George Stewart recollecting the "poison in the air" and what it did to many of those he knew (*WE*, 123). Yet such is the ambiguity of human existence that at the same time he must ask, "Was there ever a crowd like ours? Was there ever a time when so many people tried, so pathetically, to feel responsible for all mankind? Was there ever a generation which yearned to belong, so unsuccessfully, to something larger than themselves?" (*WE*, 4).

Some are literally and physically destroyed by the passions of the Thirties, like the little Ontario puritan Norah Blackwell, who is converted to communism, becomes Jerome's mistress when he goes to Spain, and throws herself under a car in Paris. Others survive for a living death, like Arthur Lazenby, the party member who had accepted communism as a religion, is disillusioned, and, suffering "utter desiccation of soul," is able to adapt himself with ease to the soulless pattern of the perfect Canadian bureaucrat.

Catherine is not unaffected by the urges of the Thirties, since they tear her husband away and disrupt the life as a normal person she has painstakingly built up, but she strives to keep apart from them.

"If only the world would leave us alone," she said, and stared out at the white land and the ink-black lake. "If only it would leave us alone our days would be a paradise." (*WE*, 219)

By the inner strength her sickness has bred, she survives Jerome's desertion and the heart attacks that follow it, and remains undestroyed. George is preserved from the kind of destruction Norah Blackwell and Arthur Lazenby suffer by the strength of his obsessive love for Catherine, which makes it impossible for him to give himself wholly to any creed, but even he feels a kind of despair at what he and his country have become. For any comparison between the Thirties and the Fifties is bound to be ambiguous. "In the bleak years we at least were not alone. In these prosperous years we were. The gods, false or true, had vanished" (*WE*, 323).

It is only Jerome who goes boldly through the agony like a legendary hero, following his long journey from the talk-fogged rooms of Canada to the sites of action, to the trenches of Spain, the prison camps of half a world, and emerges transfigured because he has suffered it all, has accepted it all, and has been purged of the guilt which the First War laid upon him. But Jerome, who is luminescent with the "cool, sweet light" of spiritual victory, no longer belongs to the world he revisits, and by the time he has walked out of the lives of George and Catherine, the very texture of the novel has changed. It is no longer the social world that concerns us; it is the inner drama for which society is only the stage.

There is a Gothic feeling about the last pages of *The Watch that Ends the Night,* embodied especially in Jerome who with his compelling eyes reminds one of so many Gothic wanderers from Melmoth to the Ancient

Mariner, and who—as they often do—imparts enlighten-
ment, so that George is able to gain or regain "a sense of
how utterly tremendous is the mystery our ancestors
confidently called God." From crying out in the Thirties,
"Anything to break the system that causes these things,
George. Anything!" (*WE*, 168), Jerome comes round in
the Fifties to preaching that truth known of all the
mystics: "You can only live again by facing death. Then
you outface it" (*WE*, 365). But the life by which you
face it is of course the spiritual life. It is to these last chapters, dominated by Catherine's illness, her almost mir-
aculous recovery, her survival as a diminished and dying
woman filled with spiritual light, that the title of course
refers—*The Watch that Ends the Night*—and there is
much in this novel of an attitude that existed in the West
before the puritans got to work and still exists in the
East today, the attitude which sees a man going into the
world and taking part in its action when he is young, and
then, as the shadows begin to gather over him, turning
inward to nurse the spiritual flame that will guide him
into the world of light.

Such insights are notoriously difficult to render into
literature and the effort to move in metaphysical realms
has not been without harm to the credibility of the characters who are MacLennan's creations. *The Watch that
Ends the Night* is rich in well-drawn, idiosyncratic and
highly convincing minor characters. George's childlike
inventor father, Dr. Bigbee of Waterloo, and Shatwell,
the assistant master who has failed in every corner of the
Empire, are thoroughly memorable comic characters in a
rather Wellsian way, while anyone who lived through the

Thirties will have met the prototypes of Norah Blackwell, Arthur Lazenby and Adam Blore.

It is when we come to the leading characters that the difficulties arise. Can Jerome, for example, be judged as a credible character in the ordinary sense? A Japanese scholar, Keiichi Hirano, has put a very interesting case for regarding him as a fictional version of Dr. Norman Bethune, the Canadian surgeon who went to work for the Loyalists in Spain and died while serving the Chinese Communists. It is possible that some of the legend of Bethune did enter into Jerome, for characters are compounded from many fragments of memory and experience, but there seems no doubt that the ultimate lesson of Jerome's life is completely different from Bethune's consistent dedication to a revolutionary ideal, and we are forced to conclude that Jerome is more important as a symbol than as a portrayal of any person in real life or even as an imaginary character, and that in him Mac-Lennan's wanderer myth reaches its greatest complexity.

George is quite another matter. There is no grandeur about him, and a great deal of ironic self-deprecation. Some critics have attacked MacLennan for creating so platitudinous a figure, but I suspect this aspect of George was deliberately done to provide a humble foil for the heroic Jerome and the queenly Catherine. Catherine is just about as near as we are ever likely to get in modern Canadian writing to the *princesse lointaine* of chivalrous romance, and her distance from the other characters and from reality is there throughout, until in the end she is shown receding from George towards death, a kind of light-filled phantom. And to this mediaevally remote lady George plays the dolourous knight, full of chivalrous notions which seem out of place except in the romances, and hence the figure of grand platitude; I think that in portraying him in this way MacLennan did present fairly faithfully a worthy and dying type of eastern Canadian.

Yet even George, the most authentic of the trio, is not convincing in the same immediate way as Shatwell or Adam Blore, and I suspect that, once again, it is due to the fact that he embodies a great deal of his creator's own life. Like MacLennan George taught for years in an English-style private school (and the resemblances between Lower Canada thirty years ago and Waterloo have yet to be explored); like him he became a radio commentator and eventually a professor. Even more important, there are close and clear parallels—upheld by certain passages in the essays—between Catherine and MacLennan's wife Dorothy, particularly in the sickness they shared and their common passion for painting. Clearly this is not the time to explore the link deeply, but it does suggest that in places *The Watch that Ends the Night* is pushed out of fictional proportion by feelings that are too direct and personal.

Still, in all, it is a notable book, perhaps the best of Canadian social novels, and, despite its imperfections, the most impressive of MacLennan's works. As for the flaws, it is as well to remember that most of them can be found in Dickens also.

XI

THE ORPHAN HEART

There is a passage in *The Watch that Ends the Night* which now, a decade after the novel's publication, seems almost pathetically ironic. George Stewart talks of a late winter afternoon at McGill, when he is about to go home with his step-daughter, Sally. As they leave he looks at her fellow students and, recollecting the Thirties, he cannot help being impressed by the happiness of their moods and their lots.

> Not one of them was corroded by the knowledge that nobody wanted them. They all expected to get jobs and marry young and to raise families young, and now as I walked down the corridor I felt joy flood me as I heard the happy noise they made at the end of the day. (*WE*, 4)

I was teaching then in a western Canadian university, and I remember no "happy noise . . . at the end of the day." Certainly, whether or not MacLennan then heard it at McGill, he has not heard it for several years, as his lectures and published essays on the student moods of the later sixties amply demonstrate; the impression one gains from these recent writings, and equally strongly from his latest novel to date, *Return of the Sphinx*, is that, far from the young not being "corroded by the knowledge that nobody wanted them," we are all, whatever our ages, subject to that corrosion. Alone among his books, *Return of the Sphinx* is a novel of total alienation, and it is impossible to extract from it the optimistic lessons which the other novels in their own special ways offer.

There are signs which suggest that MacLennan originally planned *Return of the Sphinx* as a kind of recapitulatory novel in which he hoped to gather the threads of his work up to the present, and to restate their cumulative message, only to discover, when he reviewed the recrudescent conflicts in Canada, that no such facile conclusion was in fact possible.

There is, of course, a direct filiation between *Return of the Sphinx* and *Each Man's Son*. The central figure in the more recent novel is Alan Ainslie, who was once Alan MacNeil. Again, but this time only in memory, the scenes of Cape Breton appear; and Mollie Ainslie, and the dreadful night of Archie's return, and Daniel Ainslie— that good, tortured man who made of education a substitute for Calvinist discipline. Alan, after a varied career as successful civil servant and diplomat, and later as editor of a magazine of affairs crushed out by American competition, is now a politician and a federal minister, whose aim is to achieve in the country as a whole a wedding of two cultures like that he consummated by marrying Constance, the daughter of a complicatedly inbred family of French Canadian aristocrats.

In its themes and the patterns of relationship between its characters *Return of the Sphinx* is as closely related to *Two Solitudes* as it is to *Each Man's Son*. Alan's marriage to Constance, of course, parallels the marriage of that earlier politician, Athanase Tallard, to Kathleen Connors,

112

and—like Marius and Paul Tallard—the children born to the Ainslies symbolize in differing ways the ambivalent relationship between French and English Canada.

Alan's elder child is the girl Chantal, who is innocent of any sense of division within herself or between the Canadian peoples, and so projects the views of Alan himself, who is striving to secure in Ottawa the passage of legislation establishing bilingualism in the federal civil service. While Chantal slips easily from French into English and back again, her brother Daniel is most happy speaking French, and his life carries all the implications of that choice. He is, in any case, a far more complex character than Chantal, who is one of MacLennan's wholesome and simple Canadian girls, like Sally in *The Watch* and Heather in *Two Solitudes*. Bearing the name of Daniel Ainslie, young Daniel has acquired from the Jesuits in his seminary almost exactly the same burden of guilt and the same puritanical outlook as old Daniel acquired from the Calvinists. At the same time he is the only member of the family to inherit the character and the physique—quick temper and massive shoulders—of Archie MacNeil, his real grandfather. But Daniel, unlike Chantal, feels bitterly the grievances which French Canadians expressed so demonstratively in the middle Sixties, and all his fanaticism and innate violence are channelled into rebellion, a combination of generational revolt and the revolt of his mother's people against the English they imagine to be their oppressors.

No facile solution concludes *Return of the Sphinx* as it does *Two Solitudes*. By now MacLennan has learnt that for a novelist who dabbles in didacticism it is enough to pose a question. There is no answer in *Return of the*

Sphinx, and perhaps that absence is implicit in the very mythical construction of the book. For this is the first of MacLennan's novels in which the myth of Odysseus is no longer in the ascendant. The vestiges of it remain. Alan has been a wanderer and his life a journey through many testing forms of experience, yet it has led to an inconclusive destination. For there is no Penelope at the end of this Odyssey. Constance, Alan's Penelope, has been killed in an accident of grotesque and meaningless horror, while Daniel has neutralized by separatist activities the goal of his father's desire, the hope of fulfilling his vision of a united Canada. At the end of *Return of the Sphinx*, after going through an amnesia of shame, Alan retreats from the city to his cottage in the Laurentians, where he had been happy with Constance, and with Chantal and Daniel when they were children. There he experiences a kind of epiphanous consciousness of the glory of the land.

> Looking over the lake he at last accepted that he had merely happened into all this. Constance, Chantal, Daniel, Gabriel—they and all the others had merely happened into this loveliness that nobody could understand or possess, and that some tried to control or destroy just because they were unable to possess or understand it. Merely happened into this joy and pain and movement of limbs, of hope, fear, shame and the rest of it, the little chipmunk triumphs and defeats. He believed it would endure. He thanked God he had been of it, was of it. (*RS*, 303)

This is no ending for an Odyssey and no appropriate ending for the novel MacLennan has written, since such

114

vague and facile consolations do not grow out of the violence and negation that dominate, sometimes openly and sometimes in indirect forms, the preceding pages of *Return of the Sphinx*.

We are confronted in fact by quite another universal myth than that typified in the *Odyssey*, and it is suggested rather broadly in the novel's title. The return of the sphinx means that the world lies once again in the power of the enigma. But the legend of the sphinx and its enigma is also the legend of Oedipus. I am not talking of Freudian interpretations, but of correspondences in literature between modern life and classical myths. *Return of the Sphinx* is almost obsessively involved, not merely in the fathers-and-sons pattern of antagonisms, but also in a cross-generational pattern of sexual conjunctions. Constance, we learn, was seduced at the age of fourteen by a middle-aged cousin, and Alan, to whom she tells this on their first meeting, is clearly erotically excited by the vision it arouses in his imagination. Danel's first sexual experience is with a woman old enough to be his mother. Chantal literally forces herself on Gabriel, who is not merely old enough to be her father, but is also Alan's closest friend and therefore a father substitute. "Watching his profile, Chantal realized at last that he was just as old as he had said that he was. It was then she knew she was in love with him" (*RS*, 180).

This Oedipal pattern which emerges in the sexual longings of the Ainslie children is the reaction to a sense of alienation—groups from groups and individuals from individuals—that dominates the whole of *Return of the Sphinx* and is projected in the state of orphanhood which preoccupies the characters and shapes the novel.

115

MacLennan has always made great use of the loss of parents, in violent or dramatic circumstances, as one of the key patterns of his novels. In *Barometer Rising*, Penelope's father dies violently during the explosion; in *Two Solitudes* Heather's father is killed in the war, and Paul's father dies suddenly when both are children; in *Each Man's Son* there is the violent death of both of Alan's parents, and in *The Watch that Ends the Night* Jerome's mother is murdered and his father is unknown.

In *Return of the Sphinx* the pattern of orphanhood becomes completely dominant. Almost every character of any significance is conscious of the violent loss of a parent, and such consciousness becomes a focal point for the generalized sense of deprivation all experience. Alan conceals the story of the death of his own real parents, but it is constantly in his mind, and it emerges twice at crucial points in the novel, once when Bulstrode, his political leader, reveals his knowledge of the event in order to strengthen his hold over Alan, and later when Alan himself tells Daniel the story of his boxer-murderer grandfather, a story which is fused with Daniel's own personal myth of alienation. Chantal and Daniel have both, of course, lost their mother violently, and Gabriel Fleury is still haunted by his father's death in slow agony as a result of wounds he suffered in World War I. Bulstrode, the old political veteran who has been thirty-five years in Ottawa and now at last gets his taste of power, was orphaned violently when his parents were killed in a Yukon avalanche. Marielle, the woman who is Daniel's initiatrix, saw her father killed in a naval battle at Casablanca. The separatist Latendresse was reared in a foundling home and Daniel actually talks of the French Canadians as an orphan people. The alienation, though it is given concrete and personal shape by the presence of so many orphans, extends into deeper forms; in a debate in the House of Commons Ainslie makes his recognition of it the basis of an argument one can take as the philosophic theme of *Return of the Sphinx*.

> I believe the crisis came when humanity lost its faith in man's ability to improve his own nature. If the symptoms of this disease at times seem startling in my own province, it is only because the crisis has come there so suddenly. When people no longer can believe in personal immortality, when society at large has abandoned philosophy, many men grow desperate without knowing why. They crack up—and don't know they have. (*RS*, 267)

This, of course, is the case with Daniel. He has cracked up. So, in fact, has Alan himself at the end, if we discount that inappropriate optimistic ending. And it is the crack-up that, in this context, is convincing. Chantal's happiness with Gabriel is not.

Return of the Sphinx does not lack the virtues that a high literary craftsmanship guarantees. There are passages in which the descriptive writing is exceptionally evocative; some characters, like Bulstrode and Latendresse, are very well drawn, though Daniel does not always carry conviction as a representative of the present radical generation and Chantal rarely seems likely; the dialogue for the most part is sharper and more tense than that of *The Watch that Ends the Night*. Yet *Return of the Sphinx* lacks the grand form and momentum of its predecessor,

117

and it does so, I think, because of the division in its heart between what MacLennan sees and what he wishes to see, so that he ends with an unresolved mingling of pessimism and optimism. Fundamentally, of course, the vision of *Return of the Sphinx* is as tragic as that of the first part of *Two Solitudes*. Once again, it would have been better if MacLennan had resisted the temptation to present a facile hope.

MacLennan's achievement up to the present rests, apart from his essays, on three good novels, *Each Man's Son*, *Barometer Rising*, and *The Watch that Ends the Night*, and on the earlier half of *Two Solitudes*. The lessons he has tried to teach in these books will be learnt or not, but in any case will lose their relevance as times change; his portrayal of Canadian life and the Canadian land will not, and I cannot foresee a time when he will not be regarded as Canada's best social novelist, and—for all his manifest imperfections—as one of Canada's most considerable novelists of any kind.

BIBLIOGRAPHY

A. Books by MacLennan

Oxyrhynchus. Ph.D. dissertation, Princeton University, 1935. Later published Amsterdam: Hackert, 1968.

Barometer Rising. New York: Duell, Sloan & Pearce, 1941.

Two Solitudes. Toronto: Collins, 1945.

The Precipice. Toronto: Collins, 1948.

Cross Country. Toronto: Collins, 1949.

Each Man's Son. Toronto: Macmillan, 1951.

Thirty and Three. Toronto: Macmillan, 1954.

The Watch that Ends the Night. Toronto: Macmillan, 1959.

Scotchman's Return and Other Essays. Toronto: Macmillan, 1960.

Seven Rivers of Canada. Toronto: Macmillan, 1961.

Return of the Sphinx. Toronto: Macmillan, 1967.

The Colour of Canada. Toronto: McClelland and Stewart, 1967.

B. Selected Criticism

Ballantyne, M. G. "Theology and the Man on the Street: A Catholic Commentary on *Cross Country*," *Culture*, 10 (December, 1949), 392-6.

Chambers, Robert D. "The Novels of Hugh MacLennan," *Journal of Canadian Studies*, 2 (August, 1967), 3-4.

Davies, Robertson. "MacLennan's Rising Sun," *Saturday Night,* 74 (March 28, 1969), 29-31.

Goetsch, Paul. *Das Romanwerk Hugh MacLennans: eine Studie zum Literarischen Nationalismus in Kanada.* Hamburg, 1960. 140 pp.

——."Too Long to the Courtly Muses: Hugh MacLennan as a Contemporary Writer," *Canadian Literature,* 10 (Autumn, 1961), 19-31.

Hirano, Keiichi. "Jerome Martell and Norman Bethune — a Note on Hugh MacLennan's *"Watch that Ends the Night,"* *English Literature,* Tokyo, English Number, 1968, pp. 37-61.

McPherson, Hugo. "The Novels of Hugh MacLennan," *Queen's Quarterly,* 60 (Summer, 1953), 189-98.

——. "Fiction, 1940-60," in *Literary History of Canada,* ed. Carl F. Klinck. Toronto, 1965, pp. 694-723.

New, W. H. "The Apprenticeship of Discovery," *Canadian Literature,* 29 (Summer, 1966), 18-33.

——. "The Storm and After: Imagism and Symbolism in Hugh MacLennan's *Barometer Rising,*" *Queen's Quarterly,* 74 (Summer, 1967), 302-13.

——. "Winter and the Night People," *Canadian Literature,* 36 (Spring, 1968), 26-33.

O'Donnell, Kathleen. "The Wanderer in *Barometer Rising,*" *University of Windsor Review,* 3 (Spring, 1968), 12-18.

Phelps, Arthur L. "Hugh MacLennan," in *Canadian Writers,* Toronto, 1951, pp. 77-84.

Tallman, Warren. "Wolf in the Snow," *Canadian Literature,* 5 (Summer, 1960), 7-20, and *Canadian Literature,* 6 (Autumn, 1960), 41-48.

Watters, R. E. "Hugh MacLennan and the Canadian

Character," in *As A Man Thinks*, ed. E. Morrison and W. Robbins, Toronto, 1953, pp. 228-43.

Wilson, Edmund. "Hugh MacLennan," in *O Canada*, New York: Farrar, Straus and Giroux, 1965. pp. 59-80.

Woodcock, George. "A Nation's Odyssey: The Novels of Hugh MacLennan," *Canadian Literature*, 10 (Autumn, 1961), 7-18.

——. "Hugh MacLennan," *Northern Review*, 3 (April-May, 1950), 2-10.